3.25

# *Unity and Nationalism in Europe since 1945*

# Unity and Nationalism in Europe since 1945

BY

## WILFRID KNAPP

FELLOW AND TUTOR IN POLITICS,
ST. CATHERINE'S COLLEGE, OXFORD

1966
THE QUEEN'S AWARD
TO INDUSTRY 1966

## PERGAMON PRESS

OXFORD · LONDON · EDINBURGH · NEW YORK
TORONTO · SYDNEY · PARIS · BRAUNSCHWEIG

Pergamon Press Ltd., Headington Hill Hall, Oxford
4 & 5 Fitzroy Square, London W.1

Pergamon Press (Scotland) Ltd., 2 & 3 Teviot Place, Edinburgh 1

Pergamon Press Inc., Maxwell House, Fairview Park, Elmsford,
New York 10523

Pergamon of Canada Ltd., 207 Queen's Quay West, Toronto 1

Pergamon Press (Aust.) Pty. Ltd., 19a Boundary Street,
Rushcutters Bay, N.S.W. 2011, Australia

Pergamon Press S.A.R.L., 24 rue des Écoles, Paris 5e

Vieweg & Sohn GmbH, Burgplatz 1, Braunschweig

*Printed in Great Britain by A. Wheaton & Co., Exeter*

# Contents

# *Preface*

THIS book was written at a time when Europe faced one of the many turning points in its history. A new generation had grown up after the Second World War. Young adults had been born after the fighting was over, and had no memory of the origins of the cold war, the Berlin blockade, the imposition of communist rule in Czechoslovakia or the breakaway of Tito's Yugoslavia from the Cominform.

This new generation were heirs to a Europe with a distinct personality. The cradle of a major part of modern civilization—both its technical achievement and its thought—Europe was still a small peninsula jutting out from the great land mass of Russia and Asia and pointing towards the United States. Its characteristic political achievement was the growth of the nation state; yet political boundaries had never destroyed its underlying unity.

Nonetheless, political conflicts had threatened much that was valuable in European civilization. After the Second World War western Europe faced the possibility of economic collapse and became for a time dependent on the United States, while eastern Europe was subordinated to Stalinist dictatorship. Twenty years later western Europe had regained its prosperity and for the most part enjoyed political freedom; in eastern Europe the old force of nationalism weakened the dominion of the Soviet Union over its neighbours, until in August 1968 the Russian Government ordered the occupation of Czechoslovakia by its armed forces rather than see its rule disintegrate.

Russian action gave a fresh twist to the tensions of twentieth-century Europe. The movement towards independence in eastern Europe was halted and turned back for an unforeseeable period, and the links which had begun to grow with such strength between the West and East suffered proportionately. But the underlying forces of unity and nationalism remain; it is the interplay of those forces in the twenty years after the war which this short survey attempts to describe.

*Oxford*                                                            W. K.

# CHAPTER 1

# Europe and the New World

THE end of the Second World War marked the end of an epoch in which Europe had been the centre of the world. European civilization had survived the long medieval conflicts with Islam and established its dominance by superior political organization, technological achievement, and a genius for innovation. Its achievement was not unprecedented; throughout human history successive civilizations have achieved a temporary dominance over the rest of the world, ranging from the ruthless invasions of the Mongols to the cultural pervasiveness of the Greeks. The rise and fall of civilizations has indeed been a constantly recurring theme of historical study.

In the political sphere the most recent achievement of European civilization—a product of the nineteenth and twentieth centuries—was the creation of the nation state. Like so many human achievements this was one which carried as many curses as it did blessings. The nation state was and is based on the deepest and most durable political emotion of our present civilization—that of nationalism, of the sense of solidarity with people who speak the same language, or live on the same islands, or believe they share a common heritage. Since the success and stability of government depend on the allegiance of the governed, a state whose boundaries coincide with those of a nation, and which therefore derives its authority from the emotional attachment of its people, starts off with an advantage over others. Ever since ordinary people acquired feelings and sentiments of national identity and national loyalty—ever since the French Revolution that is to say—states which have been composed of two or several separate nationalities have been weakened by rivalries between their constituent parts.

Within the framework of the nation state the arts and sciences of Europe were free to achieve their full development. A single authority had come to replace warring and rival feudal lords. Once coercive power was vested in a central authority or in clearly designated local authorities it could be used effectively to suppress banditry and crime. Property became secure—at first landed property, real and tangible in itself, and then such notional claims to property as banknotes or figures in a register. Security for capital and property meant that industry could develop, and that part of the return on capital would be reinvested to strengthen the basis of industry. At the same time new research was undertaken and the speed of technological development increased at an increasing rate. In the 1830's it took as long to travel from Rome to London as it had taken a Roman legionary; in the 1960's rockets travelled to the moon.

The arts matched the sciences in the pace of their development. The relation of artistic achievement to social and political circumstances poses more problems than can usefully be explored here, and judgement of the quality of art, whether it be a Picasso painting or a Persian ceramic, remains a matter of taste. But, regardless of individual taste, the history of European art in the modern period is distinctive, for better or worse, in the speed with which one style has succeeded another. In the last two centuries a classical style of the end of the eighteenth century gives way to the romanticism of the early nineteenth, to be replaced in turn by realism; the great revolt of impressionism was barely complete before the post-impressionists dominated the scene, their innovations in turn giving way to cubism. New materials were used for the arts as for industry, and so innovation, indispensable for industrial and social development, came to be equally prominent in painting and sculpture—where some would argue that it was less appropriate. Neither style nor material became ossified, as had so often happened in earlier civilizations.

The superiority of Europe in its political organization and material wealth was accompanied by an extension of European rule and influence over the whole world, as had always happened when one region of the world acquired a temporary pre-eminence—with this difference, that the extension of a single European culture was the work of several separate and usually rival nation states. Direct imperial rule was established in every corner of the globe, and at the same time Europe showed every other aspect of a dominant power. As in the sixth century the Emperor Justinian had sent to China to learn the secrets of silk, so in the nineteenth and early twentieth centuries men came to Europe to learn the technology and the arts of government. European artists and scholars were pre-eminent in the way in which they both sought fresh inspiration in their own past and engaged in fresh sallies of innovation and creativeness; and it was they who excavated the ancient monuments of Asia, carrying out research into the ancient history of distant lands whose indigenous art had become stultified in the repetition of traditionalism.

The achievement of Europe in the golden age of the nation state was bought at great cost. Nationalism itself was and is a two-faced genie. While providing the emotion on which the nation state could be founded and based it also fed the passions of injustice and intolerance so that minorities—including that stateless minority the Jewish people—were deprived of the rights which, by this time, were generally thought to belong to all men. Intolerant within the state, nationalism was often expansive beyond the bounds of the state; pride in one's own nation passed all too easily into scorn for others. Above all the grouping of nation states in a single continent gave rise to rivalries and struggles for mastery over the continent as a whole. In the twentieth century this struggle for mastery had given rise to the first great war of 1914–18, which was in turn followed by the worst excesses of perverted nationalism in Nazi Germany, and the second murderous conflict of 1939–45.

After the Second World War Europe ceased to be the centre of the world in two major senses. Firstly, the nationalism which had constituted its own dominant force now spread beyond the bounds of Europe, first to Asia and then to Africa. As it did so the great confidence trick of imperial rule came to an end. The relatively small countries of Europe had governed, with more or less success, peoples more numerous than themselves thousands of miles away. Sometimes their rule had been established by military victory, and was followed by material exploitation. But it had endured by bringing a system of law and order which indigenous populations accepted because it was better than the petty civil wars from which they had previously suffered, or because it was accompanied by a higher standard of living, or, most often, because it did not occur to them to join together and to agitate, even to fight with the confidence that in the end they could win and expel their alien rulers. The fact that the Japanese so easily overran South-east Asia and defeated the European rulers encouraged new aspirations amongst the Asians at the same time as it gave them new organization and new weapons; but even without the Japanese invasions they would have been aroused by the passions of nationalism as their fellow men in Europe had been before them.

The growth of nationalism was accompanied by a growth of population, and once this happened it became the exception for a European power to maintain its imperial rule over an Asian or African country. The manner with which European countries relinquished their imperial rule varied from one instance to another. The British surrendered their rule over India in response to nationalist pressure which had not yet reached the point of unremitting violence, while the French fought a seven-year war in Indo-China, to be followed by a war of equal length in Algeria, before conceding independence. But in the long run the process was almost everywhere the same: the imposing apparatus of imperial rule, with all the benefits it had conferred and all the misdoings associated with it, had rested on the assumption of power rather than its actual use. Once the numerous populations of Asia and Africa were prepared to combine to question and oppose that power it could only be maintained by a resort to force, and such force the European powers were prepared to use only in small doses and for short periods—whether because of the expense to themselves or because it appeared a hopeless and immoral task to try to subdue millions of people on the other side of the world.

This then was the first sense in which Europe ceased to be the centre of the world—it was no longer the centre of empire, as the empires themselves disappeared, or gave way to looser groupings like the British Commonwealth and the French Community. In the twenty years that followed the war, however, the change did not constitute a fundamental reversal. The disappearance of empire did not hinder European countries in the development of their own economies and societies—indeed they sometimes seemed to be better off now that they were not devoting resources to the government of an empire. They were dependent on the world beyond Europe for the supply of raw materials—and they became increasingly dependent as oil became the most important source of energy. They were sometimes jittery in consequence, lest these supplies should be cut off—as were the British when they invaded Egypt in 1956. But as the supplying countries were even more dependent on markets in the developed areas of the world, as well as for the supply of capital and technical knowledge, there was never any serious breakdown or threat of a breakdown in such supplies.

Nor did any new centres of the world emerge in Asia and Africa. The most successful modernizing country of Asia continued to be Japan. Richly endowed with the talents of adaptation and innovation, the Japanese quickly recovered from their almost suicidal war and became one of the leading industrial countries of the world. Had they been acting in concert with China they might have constructed a great new oriental civilization which, alone, they were too small to create; but China was rent by civil war and then subjected to a Communist government which succeeded in making nuclear explosions but not—in the short space of twenty years—in overcoming the more fundamental problems of a vast country and an overwhelming population. Elsewhere in the former colonial world it rapidly became apparent that while nationalist opposition could quickly overthrow imperial rule, it took very much longer to establish a successful nation state—whether it be in a vast continent like India, a widely dispersed country like Indonesia, or the tribal societies of Africa.

The rival centres of the world which emerged from the Second

World War were not therefore to be found rising from the ashes of empire. They were the great powers whom the French writer Alexis de Tocqueville had forecast in this role in the nineteenth century—Russia and America.

As late as the beginning of the twentieth century both Russia and the United States were "underdeveloped" or developing countries —although they enjoyed greater advantages than many states which are so labelled at the present time. Both were producers of primary products with comparatively little industrial development and both were dependent on a supply of capital from the outside—that is to say from western Europe, the only area of the world with a substantial surplus of capital for export.

As underdeveloped countries they were totally different from each other, and in the course of their development they continued to diverge. Russia, in 1917, exchanged old-fashioned Tsarist autocracy for a dictatorship which, over the years, developed into a stable and relatively efficient totalitarian regime. Although it did not bring political freedom to the people of Russia, the Soviet regime developed the country's industry and achieved a rate of economic growth equalled by only a few other examples in world history, such as Japan at the end of the nineteenth century and West Germany after 1949. The population, which had long exceeded that of any western European state, was educated into literacy and then provided with ample training in scientific studies and technical skills. Only agriculture lagged behind. Totally disrupted by collectivization, agriculture provided both a surplus to finance industrial development and labour, in forced labour camps, for the building of industry—at the cost of its own development. With difficulty, agricultural production was creeping back to its 1913 level when war broke out in 1939.

In the United States economic development was accompanied by an increase in the powers of the Federal government. As in other countries, government assumed powers and responsibilities for the regulation of economic and social activity which would have been totally unacceptable in an earlier generation. Legislation was passed to prevent the growth of monopoly, to regulate the price of public utilities, and then to ensure reasonable working hours and fair labour conditions. Provision was made for social security—and all this in spite of the almost universal rejection by the American people of anything that was called "socialism".

Even so, the strengthening of government in the United States took place in a constitutional manner and retained the form and the spirit of democratic government (both of which were indeed extended after the Second World War as, by slow and painful stages, democratic rights were extended to the Negro population). Although industry and agriculture were subject to state regulation of the sort to be found in all developed societies, they continued to be free-enterprise systems. The government only intervened to safeguard the minimum rights of the people, and to create conditions in which privately owned business, industry, and agriculture could operate.

By the time these two great powers were brought into the war—the Soviet Union when it was attacked by Germany and the United States when the Japanese bombed its fleet at Pearl Harbour—they had both become powerful industrial countries. Their experience of war differed sharply. The Soviet Union bore the full brunt of the German attack on its western front and suffered the loss and destruction consequent on invasion and on battles fought on its own territory. The homeland of the United States in contrast remained untouched by the war even though American forces were engaged in action all over the world rather than being concentrated on a single front. Moreover, the industrial growth of the United States, the rapid growth of scientific knowledge and technological advances made it possible to fight the war and to supply the major needs of America's allies with only a minimal deprivation on the part of the people.

Nonetheless, the two great powers were bound together by the conflict with their common enemy, Germany. In different ways the leaders of the two countries attached importance to the continuance of this alliance after the war. President Roosevelt, in his wartime conversations with Stalin, tried to establish a bond of understanding with the Soviet leader. He believed that there was much in common between Russia and America as new great powers on the world scene. He was distrustful of what he regarded as the old-fashioned imperialism of the British and the French. He thought that their concern in fighting the war was as much the preservation and restoration of their old empires as the defeat of Germany, and he supposed that he and Stalin would have a common outlook in their opposition to imperialism. He also attached great importance to his ability to get on with Stalin. He expected the United States to withdraw its forces from Europe very soon after the end of the war, and wanted to make sure, therefore, that the dominant power on the continent—Russia—would be well-disposed towards the United States.

Stalin's attitude is much more difficult to establish, because of the secrecy which still surrounds Soviet thoughts and actions—especially those of Stalin. We do know that the wartime alliance was important to him as a means of checking any renewal of German power; but it is also clear that he was intent on taking his own steps to secure Russian interests, both in reconstruction from the war and in the pursuit of security.

Moreover, the differences in the economic and political development of Russia and the United States were accompanied by even more fundamental divergences of history and outlook. The Communist Revolution in Russia, in 1917, was inspired by a belief in an inevitable historical process which would lead necessarily to the establishment of communism in all the countries of the world. Communist ideology was thus believed to be applicable to all parts of the world. The success of the Revolution in Russia was followed by the establishment of Communist parties in all the countries of Europe and many countries outside Europe—wherever it was possible for them to exist. They either were based on existing working-class organizations or were newly founded.

As the government of the Soviet Union became more institution-alized the force of ideology inevitably diminished. Moreover, the Communist parties outside Russia became dependent on the Soviet Union, and were subject to increasingly dictatorial direction from Moscow. The direction which they were given by Stalin was not one which favoured revolution. Ever since 1924 Stalin had developed the theme of "socialism in one country", implying that the first objective of the Communist world must be the safeguarding and development of communism in Russia. He manœuvred out of power those, like Trotsky, who wanted a more revolutionary policy abroad.

In spite of this the presuppositions of communism continued to be that there was an inevitable conflict between the Communist and the Capitalist worlds—neither could tolerate indefinitely the existence of the other. The conclusion which Stalin seems to have drawn from this presupposition is that Russia should advance wherever it was safe to do so, and above all should neglect no opportunity to strengthen its defensive position against the Capitalist world.

But Stalin was not only suspicious of the Capitalist world; he was at least as suspicious too of other Communists—of those who might rival his own power. The whole history of his government of the Soviet Union was of the elimination from power of all possible rivals. His insistence on "socialism in one country" was part of this —he could not afford to have foreign Communist parties capturing power and setting themselves up as rivals to the Soviet Union.

The combination of these factors made Russia a naturally expansionist power. The opportunity for expansion existed at the end of the war as Europe was freed from Nazi domination. The incentive for expansion existed too, whether it followed from the crusading belief of some Communists in the universal validity of their ideology, or the more suspicious outlook of Stalin, that if he did not take power someone else would. The means to expansion existed too: in the Soviet army as it liberated eastern Europe, and in Communists trained and organized in Moscow, ready to establish Communist governments and follow Stalin's direction.

At first sight it might appear that the United States had no ideology to compare with that of the Soviet Union, and that the American people wanted nothing other than to bring their soldiers home and live in the isolation of their own continent—this was what had happened after the First World War, and what Roosevelt expected to happen again. But in fact a great change had come over the United States since that time. Its involvement in the Second World War had been far greater than when it had come to the aid of Britain and France in 1917. Its people were aware that in the course of that war they had become a world power, and they believed that they had fought for certain ideals of freedom, independence, and the development of the world's material wealth. They had associated their religion with their own national ideals— and this was true for the Jewish Americans as it was for all the different Christian denominations. As a new nation and one that had been created out of so many different races which had emigrated to the United States they believed too that their own ideals were applicable to other countries of the world. They did not share the Communists' dogmatic belief in an inevitable historical process; but they did think that the growth of wealth through free enterprise and the establishment of democratic institutions was a natural process which, if untrammelled by government restrictions, would develop everywhere in the world.

In addition, the American people were living in a sense of shock at the disappearance of the security which their isolation had seemed to offer. They had not chosen to enter the war—but they had been brought into it by the Japanese attack. They were deeply aware that events thousands of miles away might initiate a fresh series of crises, ending with a threat to the United States itself. Their unreadiness to see the ideals of the war squandered was therefore strengthened by a sense of danger to their own security.

Finally, the United States would undoubtedly have emerged, after the Second World War, as expansionist in a non-political sense. As a developed industrial country it now had capital for export, and there was every incentive for Americans to invest and to found subsidiary companies elsewhere in the world. Their people had the resources to travel, to pursue their education abroad—to act as representatives in foreign countries, whether of their governments or industrial firms.

It is unlikely that the United States would ever have become politically expansionist as a result of this natural tendency to extend its economic and general influence. There was never any question of establishing dominion over the states of Europe, and the Americans were proud of the fact that they had fought a war for their own independence—they had no wish to begin establishing a formal empire of their own. But on the other hand isolation was a thing of the past. The number of people who now thought it possible for America to retire and withdraw into its own fortress to the neglect of the rest of the world was very small.

Between the Soviet Union and the United States stood the states of Europe. The experience of the war through which they had just passed, and the very size and strength of the new superpowers, gave the peoples of Europe a strong stimulus towards their own union. They were aware that the new eminence of the United States and the Soviet Union derived in the first place from the size of their land mass and their populations. There was a strong incentive to union as a means of rivalling the political and economic strength of the superpowers rather than seeing themselves eclipsed and unable to influence the course of world politics. They were aware too of the heavy price they had paid for the independence of nation states, emerging as they did from two great wars which had racked the continent of Europe. They looked for a new means to prevent the recurrence of the war between Germany and France, to do better than earlier peacemakers.

But at the same time Europe had already become the arena for a fresh struggle for power between the two superpowers. The struggle began with the establishment of Communist rule over the countries of eastern Europe. Where Communist rule was established, all hope of union with the West disappeared. In western Europe a fresh incentive for union was immediately created—the incentive to unite in defence against the extension of Soviet power. Some of the peoples of western Europe wanted still to unite against both the Soviet Union and the United States; but the majority saw themselves as allies of the United States against the East. It soon became obvious that it would be very difficult for western Europe to isolate itself from the United States even if it wished to do so—economically prostrate, it depended on assistance from across the Atlantic to recover from the war.

In this way the forces of nationalism and unity in Europe as the war ended were given an unexpected complexity. Nationalism was a weakened force and the incentive to unity stronger because of the war; but superimposed on this conflict was the development of the Cold War, which split the continent into east and west. It created a false unity in the east as totalitarian rule was imposed on eastern Europe, while in the West the movement towards union was intertwined with the development of an Atlantic alliance and an American presence in Europe.

The three greatest changes in the map of Europe at the end of the Second World War were the division of Germany, the westward movement of Poland—and the extension of the territory of the Soviet Union. It appeared as if Stalin deliberately aimed at the re-establishment of the old Tsarist frontiers of Russia. The Baltic states of Estonia, Lithuania, and Latvia were incorporated into the Soviet Union during the war. The Prussian port of Koenigsberg and eastern Poland were similarly integrated and so were the long-disputed provinces of Bessarabia and Bukovina. In this way the whole western frontier of Russia moved some miles further into Europe.

No attempt was made by the Soviet government to include Poland, Rumania, Hungary, or Bulgaria into the Soviet Union and it is difficult to know what expectations Stalin had formulated about the future of these countries. It is likely that he was determined above all to retain Poland and Rumania under Russian control as a barrier against future attacks on the Soviet Union and that at the same time he prepared for the possibility of this frontier zone extending further westward should opportunity occur. As a result, when Soviet armies were in occupation of Bulgaria and Hungary the opportunity was used to establish Communist control. This was not done initially by the elimination of all other political forces in these countries. On the contrary, coalition governments were established and prewar political parties revived to participate in them. Ultimate control always remained, however, in the hands of the local Communist party under the direction of Moscow through Soviet embassies and Soviet police. Then within two years of the end of the war, whether as the result of an independent Russian decision or in response to Western policies, control was tightened, opposition eliminated, and a monolithic state structure established.

The Western powers—the United States and Britain as wartime allies in particular—resisted the extension of Communist rule as far as they were able to do so. But they had no means at their disposal to counter the determination of Soviet policy or the resources at its command. In the wartime conferences between Stalin, Churchill, and Roosevelt, Churchill had constantly pressed, with support from Roosevelt, for the establishment of a Polish government including representatives of all political forces in Poland. His efforts were not entirely without success since Stalin was prepared to make certain concessions to retain the unity of the wartime alliance. But the concessions which were made were minor and of no practical significance. In the rest of eastern Europe, particularly in those states which had sided with Germany against Russia, Churchill anticipated that Russia would exercise a preponderant influence and agreed in a wartime exchange with Stalin that Russia should play the major part in immediate postwar settlement. It was never his intention, however, that Russia should be allowed to establish absolute control; while Roosevelt and his advisers had pressed successfully for the inclusion in the Yalta Declaration of a statement regarding the countries of eastern Europe, intended to guarantee their political freedom.

Verbal agreements and protests were minimal in their effect. As a result the Western powers and their peoples were confronted, as hostilities drew to a close and in the months following the war, with a series of actions on the part of the Soviet government by which non-Communist leaders in eastern Europe were thrust aside, subjected to threats, sometimes to arrest and imprisonment, while others sought safety in flight. In some ways the fate of Poland appeared the most tragic to the British people since the immediate cause of the war in 1939 had been the independence of that country from German domination; but the effect of the Hungarian Prime Minister, Ferenc Nagy, remaining in Switzerland rather than daring to return to his own country, or of the arrest and disappearance of

Petkov in Bulgaria, was scarcely less in its effect in Britain and the United States than the ousting of Mikolajezyk from Poland.

It was in Germany that the confrontation of the new Soviet empire with the Western powers was most direct and immediate.

Throughout the war common hostility to Germany had bound Britain, America, and Russia together however much they may have disagreed about postwar settlement. The war over, they occupied Germany, sharing their occupation with the French even though the French had not participated in wartime discussions on the future of Germany. They had, moreover, agreed on the general principles which were to govern their occupation policies. These had been set out in a statement at the end of the Potsdam Conference held in July 1945. The machinery for the occupation of Germany had also been established. It consisted of an Allied Control Council for the country as a whole and a Four-power Kommandatura governing Berlin, with the possibility of recourse to a Council of Foreign Ministers when agreement could not be reached in the Control Council.

The apparent harmony of views between the victors, however, concealed certain fundamental differences. The Soviet government was determined to extract large amounts of reparations from Germany both to assist its own economic recovery and to lessen the future threat from Germany. The Western powers, aware of the disastrous effects of reparations demands after the First World War, wished to avoid heavy reparations payments—although they agreed that the level of German industry should be kept sufficiently low to prevent the reconstruction of a war potential. At Yalta and at Potsdam the Russians had secured some concession to their point of view and had even persuaded the Americans to agree to a figure of 10 billion dollars of reparations payable by Germany to Russia as a "basis for discussion". It remained, however, to agree on a final amount for reparations payments, and these in turn depended on the level of industry which the four powers thought appropriate to the peaceable existence of the German people and a disarmed German state. When it came to determine this figure the British and Americans found that their experience of occupation was very different from that of the Russians and from their own expectations and intentions. The Soviet authorities in East Germany did not hesitate to extract industrial equipment of all sorts and send it home to Russia as part of reparations payments. The Western powers in contrast, although they too were ready to dismantle war industries in their own zones, found it necessary to import food and basic necessities to keep the German people at a subsistence level of living. In doing so they received no help from the Russians, who neither permitted food to be sent across their own zonal border nor were prepared to let the Germans export in order to pay for imports of food.

The result was that by the spring of 1946 the Western powers were faced with a closed border down the centre of Germany, shutting off the Soviet zone of occupation from their own and preventing the treatment of Germany as an economic unit as had been agreed at Potsdam. Unable to affect the course of events in East Germany, they therefore took the alternative course of accepting the Russian zonal border to the extent of refusing to make deliveries of reparations from their own zones to Russia, although this had been provided for at Potsdam; and they also set about the reconstruction of the zones under their own control without regard for the hopes which they had previously entertained for a joint administration, with the Russians, of the whole of Germany.

As a result the Western powers—although France was slower in this regard than Britain and America—found themselves forming a quite unforeseen alliance with the people of Germany under their control. The alliance was first seen in Berlin. There the Russians who occupied the city as the German armies were defeated had done everything possible to establish a city government under their control before the arrival of their allies. They then sought to establish political control over East Germany, including Berlin, by fusing together the Social Democratic party with the Communist party in such a way as to give control to the Communists. In East Germany there was no obstacle to this process and the Russians found leaders of the Social Democratic party ready to work with them. In Berlin, in contrast, they met with vigorous opposition which was able to flourish under four-power control. The result was that in East Germany the Social Democratic party ceased to exist in April 1946, but in Berlin it was able to oppose the newly fashioned Socialist Unity party in elections held in October 1946. Only in the Western zones of Berlin was the election freely fought. Even so, the Social Democrats won a resounding victory, winning 60 per cent of the votes to the 20 per cent of the Communists and 20 per cent of other parties. In this way a community of interest began to emerge between the Western occupying powers and the Berliners in defence against the overweening power of the Russians.

Similarly in Western Germany it rapidly became evident that whatever might be necessary to prevent a renewed German threat in the future, the immediate task was to resuscitate the economy, to provide a reasonable standard of living and to enable West Germany to export to the rest of Europe. This could only be done if the German people were prepared to work towards the same end as their occupiers and if the occupying forces for their part were willing to evoke the co-operation of the German people. By the summer of 1946 it was evident that such was indeed the policy of the British and American governments. In June a fusion of their two zones was carried out, and in September the American Secretary of State indicated that a new period had opened when he said:

> Germany must be given a chance to export goods in order to import enough to make her economy self sustaining. Germany is part of Europe, and European recovery, particularly in Belgium, the Netherlands and other adjoining states, will be slow indeed if Germany with her great resources is turned into a poor house.[1]

Nonetheless, the division of Europe and even more of Germany was something which the Western leaders would have avoided had they found it possible to agree with the Soviet Union. Public opinion in the west was even more reluctant to see the end of the old conflict against Germany followed so rapidly by the emergence of new and deeper political divisions. Again and again statesmen sought to keep alive the possibility of some form of co-operation with the Russians and they stressed the fact that both in the United

[1] J. F. Byrnes, *Speaking Frankly* (1947), p. 189.

Nations and in the Council of Foreign Ministers they were able to talk to the Soviet representatives and subject their differences to argument and discussion rather than breaking off negotiations altogether. Winston Churchill, in contrast, having in the previous decade warned his people of the threat from Germany, now drew attention in March 1946 to the iron curtain that was descending from north to south in Europe, condemned the secrecy and dictatorial nature of Russian government east of the border, and sought closer co-operation between Britain and the United States. His speech met with limited response. *The Times* expressed the mood of the majority of Churchill's own people when it condemned his criticism of the Soviet Union and said that the West had much to learn from Communist government about economic and social planning as it had much to teach in terms of political freedom.

By the summer of 1946, however, Churchill's contention was supported by growing evidence and the hopefulness of public opinion was further daunted. In Iran, Soviet troops remained in occupation of Azerbaijan (which they had entered in the course of the war in agreement with the British to guard against Nazi subversion). Only by recourse to the United Nations and by subtle negotiation did the Iranian Prime Minister succeed in persuading Iran's traditional northern rival to abandon the position it had taken up and withdraw its troops. In Paris the former wartime allies negotiated peace treaties with Germany's allies—Italy, Hungary, Rumania, and Finland. As they did so the division which had now established itself across the territory of Europe was reaffirmed day by day in the voting of the peace conference where the Soviet bloc voted invariably as one man and showed no readiness to enter into genuine negotiations in pursuit of real agreement.

It was, however, in one of the most sensitive points of traditional Russian foreign policy that sides were taken and the division of Europe most strongly affirmed in the spring of 1947. Since the end of the war Communist guerrillas in Greece had carried on a campaign of force and subversion to gain control of the country—as they would have done at the time of the liberation had no British troops intervened. The Greek government, weak politically and militarily, had continued to rely since 1944 on the support of the British and the presence of British forces to counter Communist activity. Meanwhile, across the Straits of the Dardanelles, the Turkish government resisted claims made by Stalin—identical to similar claims made by his Tsarist predecessors—for the cession of Kars and Ardahan and for participation in control over the Dardanelles. For the British government the task of supporting the Greeks became increasingly onerous as its own financial difficulties grew worse in the long, hard winter which lasted into March 1947. Ernest Bevin, as Foreign Secretary, was under pressure to reduce British commitments abroad in order to safeguard the economy and finances of the country. In March the government finally decided that no alternative course was open to them and the decision was therefore taken to withdraw British troops from Greece.

The American government was informed of this decision and saw what it now regarded as an important bastion against the spread of communism from eastern Europe into the Mediterranean area endangered. This was a radical change of view since the time in December 1944 when Congress and public alike in the United States had been severely critical of British intervention at Athens. It was nonetheless characteristic of the rapid revision of foreign policy through which the United States had passed since the end of the war. President Truman had no hesitation in offering support to Greece and Turkey and indeed to any country in the world under the threat of Communist subversion or attack. In a declaration to Congress which came to be known as the Truman Doctrine he said:

> I believe that it must be the policy of the United States to support free people who are resisting attempted subjugation by armed minorities or by outside pressures.
>
> I believe that our help should be primarily through economic and financial aid which is essential to economic stability and orderly political processes. The seeds of totalitarian regimes are nurtured by misery and want. They spread and grow in the evil soil of poverty and strife. They reach their full growth when the hope of a people for a better life has died. We must keep that hope alive.[1]

---

[1] US Senate, *Decade of Foreign Policy*, pp. 1256–7.

As British troops were withdrawn from Greece they were not replaced by Americans. But the Truman Doctrine was given substance by the passage of a Bill through Congress for economic and military aid to Greece and Turkey. In this way the difficulties in the British economy, caused in part by the harshness of the weather, had brought about American intervention in that area of Europe which Russia had always regarded as most vital to its own interests. In addition, the Truman Doctrine had enunciated, as a principle of American foreign policy, readiness to take up a position of strength against Communist attack wherever it might occur. Some three months were to pass before a second striking departure in American foreign policy deepened still further the division in Europe and opened up important and far-reaching possibilities for the cohesion of western Europe. British economic difficulties were shared for varying reasons and in varying degrees by the other countries of western Europe. Piecemeal, the United States had given aid to shore up their economies and to provide for reconstruction; but such aid had not been sufficient to break the circle of diminishing trade and increasing restrictionism. Each country found itself forced, in order to safeguard its own balance of payments, to restrict imports from the others—in spite of the fact that the cumulative effect of such restrictions was to reduce the total volume of trade on which the countries of western Europe depended for their existence. The United States had every reason to reverse this process. It had learned as a result of the war how closely its interests were bound up with those of Europe. The bankruptcy of the European economy could only affect American prosperity adversely, and in political terms it opened up the danger of a breakdown in government and the vulnerability of the European states to communism. In the two largest states of western Europe, France and Italy, the Communist party had grown greatly in strength during the war and now commanded between a fifth and a quarter of the voting strength. It seemed more than likely that if economic adversity were to continue yet more of the population would turn to communism and the task of taking over the government would thereby be made easier.

In order to safeguard its own interests, therefore, but also with a genuine sense of community with the peoples of Europe, the United States government took the bold and imaginative step of offering aid to the European countries on condition that they were willing and prepared to co-operate between themselves in their own reconstruction and the rational use and distribution of assistance from the United States. The offer was made by George Marshall, as Secretary of State, in a speech which he gave on 7 June at Commencement (the degree ceremony) at Harvard University. His speech was carefully worded. The American government had no wish to initiate a form of economic warfare against the Soviet Union and would have welcomed any possibility even at this late date of genuine co-operation across the Iron Curtain. Least of all did it wish to accentuate political divisions in such countries as France and Italy where, until a month or two previously, Communists had participated in coalition governments. On the other hand it was well aware of the danger that the Soviet Union would take up the American offer with the intention of gaining the maximum advantage for itself while at the same time wrecking American plans for co-operation in reconstruction amongst the European states.

It was with these considerations in mind that Marshall said:

> Any assistance that this Government may render in the future should provide a cure rather than a mere palliative. Any government that is willing to assist in the task of recovery will find full cooperation, I am sure, on the part of the United States Government. Any government which manoeuvres to block the recovery of other countries cannot expect help from us. Furthermore, governments, political parties, or groups which seek to perpetuate human misery in order to profit therefrom politically or otherwise will encounter the opposition of the United States.[1]

In Europe it was Ernest Bevin who took the lead in responding to Marshall's speech. He welcomed the offer in the warmest terms and immediately undertook the necessary diplomatic preparations for a meeting in Paris of those countries prepared to accept the offer and co-operate in taking advantage of it. In Moscow and in the countries of eastern Europe the offer was equally unexpected and as a result it

[1] *Decade of American Foreign Policy*, p. 1269.

caused considerable confusion. The Soviet government sent its Foreign Minister, Molotov, to participate in the discussions resulting from Bevin's initiative, which were held in Paris from 12 to 15 June. The Czechoslovak government announced its intention of accepting the offer; the governments of Poland and Rumania expressed provisional readiness to participate. Soon thereafter, however, the Soviet government decided that the advantages to be gained from any form of participation were outweighed by the risks that would be run and decided therefore to withdraw. They did so arguing that the Marshall offer implied a threat to the national sovereignty of the European states and an unwarranted interference in their control over their own reconstruction. The Soviet withdrawal was accompanied by that of Poland and Rumania in spite of the obvious welcome which their governments had given to the possibility of American aid. More striking and more foreboding for the future was the fact that Czechoslovakia, which was not occupied by Russian troops and where a genuine coalition government under the leadership of a Communist prime minister was in office, also withdrew. The Minister for Foreign Trade was in Moscow at the time and it was clear to all that the Czech decision was taken as a result of Russian direction.

It was therefore only in western Europe that the governments were free to take advantage of the American offer. In doing so they accepted, indeed welcomed, the necessity for co-operation between themselves in economic reconstruction. They opened the way for institutional arrangements and practical exchange which drew them together in a manner that would have been inconceivable before the war. At the same time the line separating them from eastern Europe was hardened and it appeared that the Soviet government had of its own volition decided to cement the division of Europe into two. That it had done so appeared more evident in the autumn when it established a Communist Information Bureau, or Cominform, made up of the Communist parties of eastern Europe (except Albania) together with the two largest western Communist parties, the French and the Italian. All over the world Communist policy became tougher and more violent. The Marshall Plan was denounced and Communist parties went over to more violent attack according to the conditions of their own countries, ranging from strikes in France and Italy to subversive activity in India and guerrilla campaigns in Malaya and Indonesia.

Faced with this situation the United States evolved a foreign policy which was to remain substantially the same over the next two decades or more. The policy was that of containment. It was outlined under the pseudonym X by George Kennan, who headed the policy-planning staff of the state department, in two articles published in *Foreign Affairs*. Containment, as the name implied, abjured any attempt to liberate areas dominated by the Communists, but expressed a determination to prevent an extension of that area. It was based on the hope that in the short term such a policy would provide the best possibility and opportunities for people living outside the Communist bloc and that in the long term the Soviet regime, constantly frustrated in its natural wish for expansion, would mellow and change into a more liberal order of government and society. The practical results of the Russian response to the Marshall Plan and the American policy of containment, taken up as it was by most of the countries of western Europe, soon demonstrated themselves in the ensuing years. The world came to live in the conditions of the Cold War. There was no longer peace in the traditional sense; on the other hand incidents and areas of tension which in previous years would certainly have flared into actual war were now contained and limited in their scope with the deliberate purpose of preventing the outbreak of real conflict. Meanwhile, behind the shield of the new American commitment to the support of western Europe, reconstruction could proceed.

At the same time the distinctive personality of Europe was for the time being submerged. Divided in two by the Cold War, it was intricately bound up with the two superpowers of the United States and the Soviet Union. In western Europe there existed a solid core of freely and democratically elected governments—in Britain, France, Belgium, Holland, Italy, Scandinavia—joined in voluntary co-operation with the United States. They depended on American aid, and their foreign policies in Europe (although not in the Far

East) were fundamentally the same as American policy. The United States therefore had no need to resort to harsh pressures or compulsion to further its interests in western Europe. It used secret funds to assist the establishment of an anti-Communist trade union movement and for other purposes. Its Central Intelligence Agency was established in 1947 to bring together all the intelligence services which had been built up during the war; but the activities of this agency in influencing events (as distinct from gathering information) were of marginal significance in western Europe. The relationship between the western European countries and the United States was thus based on free co-operation. At the same time western Europe found the way to reconstruction only in close association with its North American partner.

The circumstances of eastern Europe were very different. In no eastern European country would rule by a Communist party alone have been acceptable to a majority of the people—although in some countries, like Czechoslovakia and Bulgaria, the Communist party would have remained a strong if not dominant partner in a coalition. The governments of eastern Europe therefore depended on the Soviet Union to keep them in power; at the same time the Soviet Union was able to decide and determine the policies of those governments, meeting little effective opposition (except in Yugoslavia). This fact was important for its effect on the lives of the people of eastern Europe; it was also important a decade later when Europe began to reassert its own personality. It was then easier for western Europe to reshape its relationship with the United States than was the case east of the Iron Curtain.

# CHAPTER 2

# Reconstruction and Defence

ALTHOUGH the history of Europe before 1939 had been essentially
the history of nation states, a movement for European union had
begun in the interwar years. In 1921 a far-sighted man, Count
Coudenhove-Kalergi, had founded a "pan-Europe movement". At
that time the only other member was his wife; but in the ensuing
years it won the support of a wide range of European statesmen and
intellectuals. Then, in 1930, the French Foreign Minister, Aristide
Briand, launched a plan for European union as a means of grappling
with the problems caused by the economic slump of the previous
year. Briand also hoped that his plan would make it easier for
Germany to play a peaceful role in an organized community. But
his ideas were viewed with suspicion in England, where it was
thought that he was aiming at the restoration of French dominance
over Europe. As the political and economic crisis deepened, and
then the Nazis came to power in Germany, the plan came to
nothing.

The condition of Europe at the end of the Second World War
gave a more powerful impetus towards union than had ever existed
before. The war itself provided the first motive force to unity. The
efforts of the interwar statesmen to solve the problem of Germany's
place in Europe had failed, so that the conflict of 1939–45 seemed in
some respects a continuation of the war which had been broken off
in 1918. As far as western Europe was concerned this was a struggle
originating between France and Germany and involving the other
powers of the continent. As the apparatus of nation states and a
balance of power between them—even with the new invention of

the League of Nations—had failed to prevent the recurrence of war, it was natural that men should seek a solution to the Franco-German problem within a new framework of European unity.

Nation states had failed in another respect. The great achievement of the nation state had been (and still is) to provide security for its citizens within which they may develop the arts of peace. But in the whirlwind of German aggression from 1938 to 1941 this security had been swept aside. States had been invaded, governments overthrown. It was necessary now to reconstruct Europe; but as a fresh start had to be made, reconstruction could more usefully be undertaken on a European rather than a national scale. Men who had fought to defend national frontiers now saw that an advantage could be gained by not restoring them to their previous strength.

Governments too had to be reconstructed. The Nazi and Fascist governments of Germany and Italy were discredited and destroyed; in the countries which were victims of German invasion governments had to be remade from amongst men who had gone into exile and others who had emerged as resistance leaders at home. Here too the opportunity seemed to present itself to build a totally new government as well as reconstructing the old—to establish a government of Europe.

The impetus to European union thus stemmed directly from the Second World War. The effect of the Cold War was to strengthen still further the motives for union, where it was possible. The experience of the Marshall offer had shown the impossibility of uniting the whole of Europe; the Iron Curtain was too rigid a barrier to be broken down. But in western Europe union might be achieved. If it could, western Europe would be stronger, and could be an effective force in world politics in spite of the new importance of the United States and the Soviet Union. Defence against the Soviet Union would be more possible, and subordination to the United States less likely.

So it was that while nationalism, national pride, and attachment to national sovereignty were in abeyance in a large part of Europe, the new ideal and a new motive force for European union challenged the old basis of politics. The success of the challenge in the years to come would depend on the strength of European feeling, on the success of civil servants and statesmen in establishing an effective European government, even in limited spheres, and the extent to which this development could occur before the old forces of nationalism reasserted themselves and national sovereignty regained its pride of place.

The strength of the European movement was greatest in the centre of western Europe. In this area—France, Germany, Italy, Belgium, Holland, and Luxemburg—there was no single idea of what constituted "Europe". Different people had different notions of what constituted for them the European ideal. But in this respect the new allegiance to Europe was no different from the sentiment of nationhood. Englishmen, Frenchmen, Germans, and Italians all have widely varying ideas of what constitutes, for them, their own past and tradition.

In the same way it was possible for Catholic, conservative, and moderate people to develop an ideal of Europe appropriate to their own outlook. They traced the origins of European thought and history to the political philosophy of the Greeks and the legal inheritance of the Romans, both of which had been absorbed and transmuted by the Catholic Church. Throughout western Europe they could see the monuments of this tradition in the great cathedrals which formed such a major part of Europe's architectural heritage. In the common practice of religion and in the widespread acceptance of the value of the individual, embodied as it was in the law and custom of western Europe, they saw indisputable evidence of unity unwisely broken by the barriers of political frontiers.

This view of Europe, in which catholicism played an important although by no means exclusive part, was the more influential because of the emergence since the war of Christian Democratic parties in the three major countries of western Europe, Germany, Italy, and France. In the first two the Christian Democratic party, led by Adenauer in the one case and de Gasperi in the other, succeeded either in winning a majority or at least being a majority partner in a coalition in every postwar election. In France the Popular Republican Movement (the MRP) achieved electoral success on a scale never imagined before the war and, although never forming a majority, held the Foreign Ministry without interruption until 1954. The natural *entente* that existed between these three parties was strengthened by the fact that their leaders had all grown up speaking German as their mother tongue—Schuman as an Alsatian and de Gasperi as a Tyrolean. All three thus owed allegiance to the Europe of Charlemagne and had good reason to be reserved in their loyalty to a purely national state.

Catholics and moderates were not the only group of people who could see a common European inheritance. For others it was the revolt of the eighteenth century against obscurantism and the political power of the Church which constituted the greatest contribution of western Europe to political ideas and organization. They too might claim inheritance from the Greeks, but saw Greek political thought as having been widened and developed by the ideas of the Enlightenment and the French Revolution. Socialists went further and owed loyalty to the international Socialist movement of the late nineteenth and early twentieth centuries. These were ideals which differed very much from those of the Christian Democratic parties. But whereas these differences had frequently given rise to conflict within national communities—and continued to do so—they did not prevent an alliance being formed in pursuit of the common objective of European union. The problems which had most worried Catholics and anti-clericals—such questions as the role of the Church in education and the rights of the clergy in a lay state—were not the concern of European political union and therefore were not a cause of dissent. Similarly the old battle between the supporters of collectivism and the adherents of free enterprise could be postponed and a fresh start made in political thinking about questions of planning under a supranational authority.

Divergences of view about the nature of the European inheritance were accompanied by differences of opinion about the part of Europe in the new world. There were many who looked for partnership between Europe and the United States. Their response to the growing threat from the Soviet Union was to attach increasing importance to an alliance between a strong western Europe and the United States and they were aware of the political advantages in economic and defence support which such an alliance would bring. This view was not, however, universally shared. The prevalent desire of all Europeans to avoid another war led many people to look for some way of contracting out of tension and conflict between the United States and the Soviet Union. Such people looked for a "third force" in Europe. The use of the word "force" was, however, scarcely justified, for the reason for contracting out was that Europe was too weak to prevent itself being overrun and could best hope for salvation in a form of neutralism which would offer the least incentive to attack. This view of a neutralist Europe was most commonly found on the left in European politics but it also had its supporters amongst moderate and conservative people and found its most cogent advocate in the influential French newspaper *Le Monde*.

The outcome of these divergences of view was the growth in the countries of western Europe of different organizations pursuing the common cause of European union, and subordinating their differences to that common end. In Britain the United Europe movement was organized under the chairmanship of Winston Churchill and had strong support from Conservatives, while coming under heavy criticism from the Labour government. In France a comparable body was the *Conseil Français pour l'Europe Unie*. Side by side with this body there existed the *Mouvement Socialiste pour les États Unis d'Europe* with strong support in Luxemburg and Belgium as well as France (where its outstanding leader was André Philip). Progressive Catholics formed *Les Nouvelles Équipes Internationales*, of which the strongest membership was in France and Belgium. The already existing European Union of Federalists grew to unprecedented strength and was particularly well supported in Italy; more specialist in its approach was the Economic League for European Cooperation, of which Paul van Zeeland of Belgium became chairman.

These and similar groups were well placed to bring pressure to bear within the governments of western Europe. They made no claim to be mass organizations and did not attempt to establish a mass base for themselves. But they included in their membership large numbers of parliamentarians and members of governments. They were no longer, as had so often been the case in the interwar years, groups of enthusiasts trying to persuade governments to relinquish part of their authority. They now included and were led by members of those governments who were able to see a role of growing importance for themselves in a larger political union in Europe.

From the beginning of the movement for European union its greatest strength was in the countries which eventually joined in the European Coal and Steel Community and the Common Market—the central core of western Europe. On the periphery Greece and Turkey, although most directly affected by the new threat from the Soviet Union, were geographically remote from the centres of industry and population in the west. Switzerland and Sweden continued to pursue the policy of neutrality which had stood them so well during the war, and this limited their readiness to join with other European states in the context of the Cold War. In the Iberian peninsula, Spain was regarded as an outcast because of its system of government, the part which Germany and Italy had played in the establishment of the Franco regime, and the assistance which Franco had given to Germany on the eastern front. The Spanish government for its part was too proud to seek respectability by the standards of the rest of the world. The interposition of Spain made it difficult for Portugal to form close links with the centre. Amongst the Scandinavian states Sweden, as we have seen, gave first priority to neutrality; Finland retained its independence from the Soviet Union on the understanding that it would not enter into any anti-Soviet coalition; while Norway and Denmark felt themselves to be remote from the historical and cultural traditions of the heartland of western Europe.

Most important of the countries on the periphery of Europe was, however, the United Kingdom. Great Britain had not shared the experience which was so important in promoting the desire for union amongst its neighbours. It had not suffered defeat; on the contrary at the most tense moment of its history it had stood alone

in Europe supported only by the members of the Commonwealth·
There was no break in its continuity with the past of the sort which
the Nazi and Fascist regimes had created in Germany and Italy.
Here again the appeal which Winston Churchill could make in a
moment of grave crisis was that this should be the pinnacle of a
thousand years in the history of the British Commonwealth. The
government of Britain had been one of coalition and national unity
for the greater part of the war. There had been no conflict of loyalty
of the kind experienced by Frenchmen and no tensions of the sort
that existed between *emigré* governments and resistance movements
on the continent.

In the course of its history Britain had always stood outside the
main course of European politics. Depending for its livelihood on
worldwide trade and relying for its security on the strength of the
fleet, it had remained aloof from the quarrels of the continental
European states. When a major upheaval occurred on the continent
the British intervened and did not rest until a peace safeguarding
their interests had been secured. Once this goal was achieved they
withdrew again from Europe, declining to take an active part in
peacetime diplomacy even when their failure to do so might open
the way to a new war. After the Second World War Britain did not
retire into isolation as it had done before. British troops remained in
Germany and the British government signed treaties in 1947, 1948,
and 1949 which committed them to the defence of western Europe
—a commitment which they had previously always refused to
undertake in peacetime. But this new departure in British foreign
policy was scarcely proportionate to the change of atmosphere in
European politics or even to the increased speed of communications.

Several of the European states were now prepared for close
political union, far more intensive than treaties of alliance. And
London would soon be only an hour away from Paris by passenger
plane. On the continent of Europe those who had looked to Britain
for leadership in the war against Hitler now hoped for similar
leadership in the reconstruction of Europe. British Conservatives
were sensitive to these hopes. Their leader, Winston Churchill,
was one of the greatest inspiratory forces of European union. In

September 1946, at Zurich, he sounded a clarion call for the unity of Europe when he said:

> We must build a kind of United States of Europe. . . .
>
> The first step in the re-creation of the European family must be a partnership between France and Germany. . . .
>
> The first practical step is to form a Council of Europe. . . . In all this urgent work, France and Germany must take the lead together. Great Britain, the British Commonwealth of Nations, mighty America, and I trust Soviet Russia—for then indeed all would be well—must be the friends and sponsors of the new Europe and must champion its right to live and shine.[1]

Even so, Churchill and his colleagues set limits on the extent to which they would abandon British sovereignty in the cause of European union. And Churchill, in opposition, could not determine the course of events. Attlee's Labour government showed an attitude of cool reserve both to grand and seductive ideas about a future union of Europe and towards any suggestion that Britain should surrender sovereignty over its own affairs. It was true that Ernest Bevin leaped at the opportunity of European co-operation offered by the Marshall Plan. On 22 January 1948 he went even further when he said:

> The free nations of Western Europe must now draw closely together. How much these countries have in common. Our sacrifices in the war, our hatred of injustice and oppression, our Parliamentary democracy, our striving for economic rights and our conception and love of liberty are common among us all. . . . I believe the time is ripe for a consolidation of Western Europe.[2]

Nonetheless, his belief, shared by his colleagues and the greater part of the Labour party, was that progress could be made in Europe by co-operation of a strictly practical kind between governments. In the long run such co-operation might lead to the establishment of European institutions and to some kind of political union. But such union not only was unnecessary to meet the practical needs of the present but would actually serve as a distraction from the solution of immediate problems. The outlook of Bevin and those who shared

[1] *The Sinews of Peace* (1948), pp. 198–202.
[2] *RIIA Documents* (1947–8), pp. 210–11.

his view was affected by the discouraging experience of politics in France, Germany, and Italy. Only in France amongst these three countries had parliamentary institutions survived in the interwar years and even there they had been characterized by the instability and ineffectiveness of government as a multiplicity of parties disputed with each other the spoils of office. In the face of this experience there was a natural reluctance in Britain to believe that European political institutions would be successful where the institutions of the main constituent countries had fallen so markedly short of success.

There were other reasons which made the Labour government reluctant to relinquish control over its own affairs. It stood out as a unique example of a Socialist party which had actually acquired power and formed a government of its own without recourse to coalition. It was in a position, therefore, to introduce the reforms it thought desirable and it was also under the imperative necessity of controlling its own economy in a time of shortage and crisis. It was the more reluctant, therefore, to abandon any part of its own governmental authority. Nor did the Labour party see itself as closely linked to Europe. It was suspicious of Conservative elements on the continent which it regarded as reactionary in a way in which the British Conservative party was not, and in spite of left-wing feelings about American capitalism, saw a closer affinity with the United States of the New Deal than with European states.

The growing tension of the Cold War brought a closer participation of Britain in defensive preparations in Europe. Even this, however, was not accompanied by greater acceptance of the European ideal. Ernest Bevin was well aware that western Europe could not be defended against the Soviet Union without the support of the United States. In his mind, therefore, the essential requirement was to keep a bridgehead for the United States in Europe rather than to unify Europe in such a way that the United States might be tempted to leave Europe to look after itself. Added to the traditional links between Britain and the Commonwealth this emphasis on the special relationship with the United States was a new force restricting the British commitment to Europe.

While Britain was thus placed in a special position with regard to Europe there were other considerations of a quite different sort which might have placed a brake on West Germany's participation in European unification. There were natural hesitations in the countries which had been overrun by Germany in the war in accepting Germany as an equal partner in Europe. These hesitations were, however, set aside until it came to the possibility of rearming Germany when they were almost strong enough to break the movement to European union. In West Germany itself doubts and decisions arose as the German people were torn between a readiness to resume a full and equal partnership in western Europe and a desire to achieve the reunification of Germany. Any movement towards the integration of West Germany into western Europe had the result in the short run of strengthening the division in Germany, however much the supporters of such a policy might argue that in the long run a strong western Europe would be an attraction to the countries under Communist rule. Stalin was aware of the sensitivity of the Germans to this fact and used every resource of propaganda therefore to offer hopes of reunification once Western union was abandoned.

The possibility of reunification was taken up in West Germany by the Social Democratic party under the leadership of Kurt Schumacher. Social Democrats were naturally opposed to the conservative elements, particularly to the alliance of Christian Democrat parties in France, Italy, and Germany, which they saw as the main protagonists for European union. They were to some extent hostile towards the former victors over Germany because of the latter's failure in their eyes to take account of the extent to which German Social Democrats had been the opponents of Nazism. They were also aware that they had been unsuccessful competitors with the Nazis in the 1930's because of the appeal which the Nazis had made to German nationalism. Now, after the war, they themselves embraced the cause of national unity, urging that the integration of the West would be a barrier to conversations with the Russians and to the possibility of achieving such unity through negotiation.

Other obstacles of a more minor kind arose between France and

Germany over the territory of the Saar, which had been in dispute between the two countries since 1870. As so often happens in human affairs the French and the Germans found it easier to talk in large terms about the desirability of Franco-German reconciliation rather than to achieve a practical settlement of a long-standing irritant between the two nations. In the course of a decade, however, it proved possible to overcome all these difficulties. The question of the Saar was settled in 1956, by which time West Germany had been accepted as an equal partner in western Europe. Vigorously as the Social Democrats pressed their case they failed to win an election and were therefore in no position to influence the course of events.

The wish to retain control of national policy and national institutions was thus strongly felt in the special case of Britain, while West Germany had special reasons for attaching importance to the hope of negotiations with the Russians. These attitudes, which ran counter to the movement for union, were present in modified form in the other European countries. It was not only in Britain that anxiety was felt that France might be looking for an escape from its own problems in the concept of European union. The Radical Party leader Pierre Mendès France, who became Premier in the crucial year of 1954, urged that his country should first meet its own political and economic needs before venturing on a larger framework. National pride too was strongly felt in France and, as we shall see, became a decisive factor when it was proposed that the French army should be subordinated to a supranational authority. In Holland reluctance to accept the principle of supranationality was felt in the same form as it was in Britain and the Dutch attached great importance to the British participating in any form of European union if they themselves were to surrender control over their own affairs.

In spite of the special position of Britain and Germany and the hesitations felt in other countries, the motive force of European union continued to gather momentum. Important questions were still unresolved—whether Europe should aim at becoming a genuine Federal union or whether it should remain more akin to a confederation. It was also questionable whether most progress would be made by the establishment of institutions with widespread but limited authority or whether it was better to give strong power to a supranational authority in a limited sector in the expectation that the sector could later be widened. But the fact that these questions remained open did not prevent progress taking place. Meanwhile, certain important steps had been taken to meet the practical needs of reconstruction and defence in Europe. The Marshall offer to Europe was conditional on the European countries co-operating amongst themselves in their own reconstruction. To facilitate such co-operation the countries of western Europe set up a permanent international body called the Organization for European Economic Co-operation (OEEC).

The result was that in the middle of the ferment of ideas about the construction of a new Europe, and while voluntary organizations and pressure groups were gathering strength, the first of Europe's new institutions came into being. OEEC was essentially inter-governmental in character. It worked through meetings of representatives of national governments. Its membership embraced all the western European countries except Spain, and it would have been difficult to establish institutions of a supranational character over such a wide area. Moreover it was established to meet the practical need of European reconstruction through Marshall Aid, and its immediate tasks were too pressing to permit any radical institutional development in the early days.

The directing body of the Organization was a Council made up of representatives of member governments. Some two or three times a year the representatives on the Council were ministers of member countries; for the rest of the time the Council was composed of officials. In this way decisions could be reached by responsible member governments at periodic intervals and in the meantime the constant meeting of officials made it easy to implement ministerial decisions and to prepare for the next round of decisions.

Just as the breadth of membership and character of the work of OEEC determined its intergovernmental character, so its dependence on the United States for Marshall Aid meant that in this respect European co-operation was closely linked to the United States. The American government set up a special branch of its own administration, called the Economic Co-operation Administration, to administer Marshall Aid, but it insisted that detailed planning should be the responsibility of the European states.

The impact of Marshall Aid on the economies of western Europe was immediate and far reaching. By supplying food, raw materials, and then an increasing proportion of investment goods such as machines and machine tools, the United States provided the basic means for recovery. Thereafter it might have been possible for the European countries to plan their investment and so build a unified economy. In fact little such planning was undertaken under the aegis of OEEC. But the increase in production and the cushioning effect of Marshall Aid funds made it possible for the OEEC countries to dismantle the trade barriers and quotas which they had established between themselves. It was in this field, in the liberalization of trade and the provision for multilateral payments, that the greatest degree of co-operation was achieved.

As the reconstruction of western Europe proceeded, Communist control over eastern Europe was strengthened and tightened. In 1946 peace treaties had been signed with Germany's wartime allies and satellites in eastern Europe, and this removed the last vestige of direct Western supervision of political events. At first the degree of Communist control had been strictest in Poland, Rumania, and East Germany; but in 1947 and 1948 it moved westwards. The negotiations with the Russians over the Marshall Plan in June 1947 coincided with fresh protests from the Western powers to Russia over the way in which the Hungarian government had been re-modelled to increase Communist power.

The most dramatic development came in February 1948 in Czechoslovakia. The Communist party was the largest party there after the war, and headed a democratically elected government. But fresh elections were to be held in May, and it was generally thought that as a result of events in neighbouring Communist countries, as well as the direction which the Soviet Union had insisted on giving to the Czechs to reject the Marshall offer, the Communist vote would fall. It was expected that they would still be strong enough to be included in the government, but not to lead it.

In the face of this possibility the Communists decided to act to forestall the elections. Taking advantage of a political crisis provoked by the action of the Communist Minister of the Interior in packing the police with Communists, they carried out a *coup d'état* and established what proved to be a Communist government. Initially the Czech Communists pretended that no essential change had been made and that their action was merely an extension of the responsibility which they had already exercised as the leading party in a coalition government. Few people were deceived by this pretence, and it was soon abandoned.

The role which the Russians played in the Czech *coup d'état* is still not clear. It was an essential part of Stalin's dominance of the Communist world that national Communist parties, the Czechs like all others, should be under direction from Moscow. Moreover, the Russian Minister Zorin, who had previously been ambassador to Prague and therefore a normal channel for Russian instructions, was in Prague at the time of the crisis. To whatever degree the Russians were involved their motives are also uncertain. Was the move long premeditated, or was it a result of a decision rapidly taken in the growing pace of the Cold War? Did it result from a determination to press Communist power as far forward as it was safe to do so, or was it a defensive move to eliminate a wedge pushing eastwards into Communist Europe?

Whatever the answers to these questions there is no doubt about the impact of the Czech *coup d'état* on the politics of western Europe. Its effect was no less because many people still felt a sense of guilt over the betrayal of Czechoslovakia in September 1938, and saw the loss of Czechoslovakia to the East as an indirect result of this desertion in face of the threat from Germany. Appeasement was totally discredited and there was widespread support for a policy of resistance.

Not that there was any obviously appropriate means of preventing similar *coups* taking place in other European countries since they were not assisted by any overt interference, far less by armed attack, from the outside. The approach of elections in Italy in May was viewed with special alarm in this respect because of the size of the Italian Communist party.

Nonetheless, some organization for defence was called for—and Ernest Bevin had given the lead to closer association between the states of western Europe in his speech in January. His initiative met with a response rendered more urgent by the Czech *coup*. In March 1948 a treaty, called the Brussels Treaty, was signed between Britain, France, Belgium, Holland, and Luxemburg. It was an important new departure. The transition from the anxieties of the war and its aftermath to the new Soviet threat was indicated by the fact that Germany was named in the text of the treaty as a possible aggressor, even though the central article, in which the signatory parties pledged themselves to mutual support in the event of attack, was obviously directed against the Soviet Union.

In another respect too the treaty was an innovation. Its article VII provided for the creation of a Consultative Council "which shall be so organized as to be able to exercise its functions continuously". This represented more than a traditional treaty of alliance. The council was to provide for continuous preparation for common defence, and regular consultation in the field of foreign and defence policy.

Important as the Brussels Treaty was, it could not provide the physical means of providing defence in Europe. Britain had disarmed, the French army was small, the economy of western Europe was only just beginning to recover under the stimulus of the Marshall Plan. The resources for defence could only come from the United States. The readiness of the United States to furnish such resources was made clear. The days when the Americans had distrusted Churchill's firmness towards the Soviet Union—when President Roosevelt had wanted to avoid giving the appearance of "ganging up" against Stalin—these days were passed. A month after the signature of the Brussels Treaty the Senate of the United States passed a resolution bearing the name of the Republican leader, Senator Vandenberg, expressing the support for any joint measures of defence undertaken by the European powers. The success of the

Vandenberg Resolution demonstrated the bipartisan following which Truman commanded in commitment to Europe.

Only a short time was to pass before the United States was fully involved in the defence of one of its key positions in Europe. As an essential step in the recovery of West Germany the Western powers had introduced currency reform into their own zones and had entered into discussions with the Russians to devise an agreed plan for such reform in Berlin. These discussions made little progress and towards the end of June the Russians introduced their own reformed currency into Berlin, following this move by an absolute restriction on communications between Berlin and West Germany. Few people in the West imagined that it would be possible to supply Berlin while the Russian blockade continued. But the Western governments were determined not to negotiate under duress and therefore initiated an airlift to give themselves manœuvring space in which to reopen discussions with the Russians. As autumn passed into winter, however, it soon appeared that on the one hand such negotiations would be fruitless and on the other that Berlin could be adequately supplied from the air. A stalemate was thus reached. The Western governments undertook no measures of force to break the blockade (although the French occupation authorities did go as far as blowing up the Russian radio station in their zone) and the Russians for their part made no attempt to shoot down any of the planes engaged in the constant traffic to and from Berlin.

British and French planes participated in the airlift but its success was assured only because of the overwhelming contribution made by the United States. It was logical, therefore, that the initiative undertaken in the Brussels Treaty and the Vandenberg Resolution should be taken a step further in the formation of an alliance between the United States and its neighbour Canada on one side of the Atlantic and the western European powers on the other. In March 1949 the North Atlantic Treaty was signed.

Like the Brussels Treaty (which it largely superseded) the North Atlantic Treaty established a Council and an elaborate civilian and military organization, which came to be conveniently referred to as NATO. Like OEEC and the Brussels Treaty Organization, NATO too was intergovernmental in character. It did not involve any formal abandonment of national sovereignty. Its governing body, the Council, reached decisions by unanimity—although actual votes were avoided as far as possible. There was a strong Anglo–American element in NATO—the methods by which decisions were arrived at in the Council were similar to those of the British Cabinet, and the unified military command which was established followed a tradition established in the Second World War, when there were Anglo–American joint chiefs of staff. The first Secretary General, Lord Ismay, came from Britain and the Supreme Commander in Europe (Salew) was an American. In the early years, while France was preoccupied with the war in Indo-China, Britain, the United States, and Canada provided the main force of active troops on the continent of Europe. The fact that the military planning was headed by a "Standing Group" composed of representatives of France as well as the United States and Britain only mitigated this element of an Anglo–American special relationship.

Although no decisions could be taken in the NATO Council against the opposition of any member, it was inevitable that, as NATO developed, member countries would be committed by decisions in the Council, and their defence forces would become enmeshed with those of other members. The presupposition of NATO was that defence, to be successful, must be collective. This meant that basic needs for a defence force—aerodromes and pipelines, communications systems—were built for common use by several member countries, with a sharing of cost between them. National forces were placed under NATO command. A NATO staff was created, and both the civilian and the military side of NATO were permanent. This meant that although the Council only met periodically as a council of heads of government, or foreign or defence ministers, it had a continuous existence as a meeting of deputies. In this way the staff of NATO acquired a loyalty of its own, independent of national governments—the military representatives indeed established themselves in New York in order to be free from the pressures of national governments which tended to concentrate on the Council's headquarters in Paris. Only fifteen years later did the

French government, led by General de Gaulle, refuse any longer to accept integration, which in their view was a cloak for American dominance.

Meanwhile co-operation in conventional defence made steady if slow progress. It did so under the umbrella of the American atomic bomb. Initially the only delivery system for the bomb was the United States Strategic Air Command. Later, atomic weapons could be delivered by missiles, or fired from cannons. The ultimate control over atomic weapons remained in the hands of national governments (the American, the British and the French). NATO did not become strong enough, politically, to control nuclear weapons of its own.

By the spring of 1949 major achievements had thus been secured in the realm of practical co-operation in Europe. In certain important respects, however, these achievements fell far short of the wishes and intentions of those who looked for closer union. The movement towards such union therefore retained its own autonomous strength and in 1949 and 1950 produced yet other institutions of a different and distinctive kind.

# CHAPTER 3

# *European Union*

IN MAY 1948 the efforts and activities of the voluntary organizations formed to promote European union reached a climax when a Congress of Europe met at The Hague. The Congress was attended by some 750 delegates, many of whom were members of the parliaments and governments of the European countries—they included Alcide de Gasperi, the Prime Minister of Italy, Jean Monnet and Georges Bidault from France, Paul-Henri Spaak and Paul van Zeeland from Belgium. Winston Churchill was Honorary President, and expressed the ideals of European union in his opening speech when he said:

> We shall only save ourselves from the perils which draw near by forgetting the hatreds of the past, by letting national rancours and revenges lie, by progressively effacing frontiers and barriers which aggravate and congeal our divisions, and by rejoicing together in that glorious treasure of literature, of romance, of ethics, of thought and toleration belonging to all, which is the true inheritance of Europe, the expression of its genius and honour; which by our quarrels, our follies, by our fearful wars and the cruel and awful deeds that spring from war and tyrants we have almost cast away.[1]

He expressed his regret at the inability and failure of the countries of eastern Europe to participate in the Congress, and reaffirmed that "We cannot aim at anything less than the union of Europe as a whole".

The delegates to the Congress were divided between those who wanted to solve specific problems before moving on the large-

[1] *The Times*, 8 May 1948.

scale creation of a European union, and those who wanted to move immediately to something approaching a Federal state. Amongst the latter was Paul Reynaud, who had sought unsuccessfully to rally France against the German invasion in 1940. Attacking those who wanted to "make haste slowly" he said: "That is all right for a man walking along a road, but not for a drowning man—and Europe is drowning." His appeal for rapid action did not command majority support; but the Congress nonetheless approved unanimously a resolution declaring that: "the time has come when the European nations must transfer and merge some portion of their sovereign rights so as to secure common political and economic action for the integration and proper development of their common resources."[1]

The Hague Congress was different from any other meeting designed to promote a political ideal in that it expressed views in accordance with the policies and intentions of several governments. Two months later the French government proposed, in the Council of the Brussels Treaty Organization, the establishment of a European parliament. The British government resisted this suggestion and proposed instead that a ministerial council should be set up, intending that within such a council governments should retain their sovereign authority and not be subject to pressures from delegates without governmental responsibility. The British countermove was not, however, strong enough to stem the tide towards union amongst the other European countries. As a result a compromise proposal was agreed amongst the Brussels Treaty powers whereby there should be created a Council of Europe consisting of a Consultative Assembly and a Committee of Ministers.

This arrangement was embodied in the Statute of the Council of Europe, which was duly signed in May 1949—one year after The Hague Congress. The movement for union had borne fruit, and a European Assembly was brought into existence. At the same time the caution of those who wanted to safeguard national institutions and national interests was embodied in the new institutions.

Representatives to the Consultative Assembly were not popularly elected but were chosen in various ways by the governments and

[1] *The Times*, 11 May 1948.

parliaments of the countries from which they came. At first the Assembly could only discuss matters referred to it by the Committee of Ministers, or for which the Committee's consent had been obtained—although this limitation was modified in 1951. Partly because of the British attitude, and also with the intention of opening the Council of Europe to neutral countries, questions of defence were initially excluded from the agenda of the Consultative Council.

These limitations on the Council's power and the fact that it could not develop into a more supranational body against the opposition of Britain and its supporters did not prevent the first meeting of the Council, held at Strasbourg in August 1949, from being an occasion of stirring and historic importance. For the first time a genuine assembly had been created representing the large majority of the countries of western Europe and devoted to the elimination of national differences and the pursuit of common European objectives. The mood of the occasion was well expressed by the French Socialist leader, Guy Mollet:

> It is indeed a family gathering which we are holding here; but there are all kinds of family gatherings. They may be for funerals as well as births. It is for us to decide whether we are here in order to bury Europe, or to give birth to Europe. I beseech you, my dear colleagues, to let it be the birth of the United States of Europe which we are celebrating today.[1]

Harold Macmillan as one of the British delegates was sensitive to this mood and declared: "It may well be that future historians will agree that this meeting of the Council of Europe was the turning point of the twentieth century. . . . Let us never again use the word impossible. We are doing the impossible."[2]

There were few dissentient voices, but the Labour representatives from Britain were chief amongst them. Herbert Morrison expressed characteristic scepticism when he pointed to the dangers of "slogan-mongering" and said "new ideas don't frighten me, I just want to know what the new ideas are and what they mean".

In the face of the reluctance of Britain and others to see their

[1] Council of Europe, Consultative Assembly, *Reports*, Vol. 1, p. 161.
[2] *Ibid.*, p. 125.

national sovereignty merged in any European institution there was inevitably a sense of anticlimax when the Council tried to add practical achievements to the bare fact of its existence.

The most striking of these practical achievements was the conclusion of a European Convention of Human Rights which was a rejection at once of the old tyranny of Nazism and the new threat to individual liberty from across the Iron Curtain. The Council of Europe was not alone in drawing up a charter of this sort since the United Nations had taken similar action. The Council went a stage further than the United Nations, however, in setting up a Court and a Commission designed to make possible the enforcement of the convention.

The Council was able to reach agreement on other conventions which had practical rather than political importance, such as the equivalence of university entrance requirements, and on extradition. More important, however, than these specific conventions was the fact that the Council provided a forum for the development of European ideas. Representatives at Strasbourg met with each other and established contacts which transcended their national loyalties. As they did so they grouped themselves together according to political allegiances rather than nationality, and in this way embryonic European political parties could be seen, even though they lacked the base of popular election and could not compete for real power. In this activity British Conservative representatives played a full part; for example Sir David Maxwell Fyfe (later Lord Kilmuir) was Chairman of the Commission on Human Rights. The participation of these representatives of the Opposition in Britain to some extent, however, gave a misleading impression. It added to the part already played by Winston Churchill in suggesting to the Europeans that when a Conservative government came to power in Britain it would revise fundamentally Britain's attitude to European union. For reasons which we shall examine later this proved not to be the case.

Important as the Council of Europe was in propagating the idea of European union, it still provided no better jumping-off point for specific plans of a supranational kind than did OEEC, and those who sought a development of this kind had therefore to make a fresh start. By the beginning of 1950 several factors encouraged them to do so. One of these was the attitude of the British government. Many people in Europe who themselves wanted to proceed as rapidly as possible towards a federation were prepared to hold back in order to ensure British participation. They argued that however desirable federation might be in itself, Europe could not be made without Britain and that a confederation with Britain was better than a closer union without. The frigidity of the Labour government towards any form of European union which went further than co-operation between governments destroyed this case. If Britain were not prepared to join a European union there was nothing to be gained by delaying the establishment of a supranational authority since every year that passed in which national governments re-affirmed their old status and importance would make such a move more difficult.

The second factor was of particular concern to France. We have seen that the French government was reluctant to join with the British and Americans as they revised their policy towards Germany in 1946. At that time the French found they had much in common with Russia, their traditional ally against Germany, in being more fearful of German recovery and wanting therefore tight restrictions on German reconstruction. Together with the Russians they advocated four-power control over the industries of the Ruhr. But by 1947 it was obvious that four-power control was unsuccessful everywhere in Germany, and that in any case the French could do nothing to prevent the British and Americans allowing the reconstruction of German industry in their own zones.

They nonetheless continued to attach importance to some form of control over German heavy industry with all its potentiality for war production. It was no longer possible to hope that such control could be imposed from the outside; the alternative was to establish a supranational authority in which Germany would participate.

Such a proposal could only hope for success if France was ready to subordinate its coal and steel industry to the same authority on equal terms. But there were a sufficient number of men in the French government who saw real and great advantages for France and for Europe in such a step. Amongst others these included men like Jean Monnet, who had been responsible for the French plan for postwar reconstruction. To them it was obvious that the industrial area around the frontiers of France, Germany, Belgium, Luxemburg, and Holland was a single economic unit and an obvious common market once political divisions could be removed. The prosperity of the region would be greatly enhanced if it could be developed as a whole and not in separate national parcels. More than that the success which such development promised would provide an admirable starting point for a wider scheme of European union. Here was the "sector" approach to unification in its most attractive form—a limited area in which supranational authority could show success and thereafter be extended to other parts of the political economy.

The Germany with which they had to deal was now quite different from that of 1947. The Berlin blockade had rendered final the division of Germany into two. Berlin was divided—henceforth when the Western powers talked of safeguarding Berlin they meant only West Berlin, not the whole of the city. The blockade came to an end in May 1949; but while it was still in progress America, Britain and France had reached agreement on a constitution for West Germany, and on the provisions of a law to govern its relations with themselves, providing for the continuance of certain controls and for occupation forces. In 1949 these agreements were brought into effect; the German Federal Republic came into existence, and Konrad Adenauer was elected its first Chancellor. Shortly afterwards—in October 1949—an East German state, the German Democratic Republic, was established by the Russians and the Socialist Unity party of East Germany.

The leadership of Konrad Adenauer in West Germany—which was to last until October 1963—enhanced the possibilities of developing European institutions. Adenauer was a former protagonist for the cause of European union. He also saw the advantages which would accrue to Germany if it entered into close co-operation with the West and particularly with the victors over Nazi aggression who were its closest neighbours. To this end he had himself opened discussions with the French government about the possibility of Franco–German collaboration in the steel industry.

The French government could therefore be confident that any proposal which it made for such co-operation would receive at least a sympathetic response in Germany. At the beginning of May 1950 Schuman, the Foreign Minister, put forward specific proposals which were to lead to the establishment of supranational institutions governing the coal and steel industry. This was the Schuman Plan and it developed from a proposal of the French government of 9 May 1950, expressed in these terms:

> To place Franco–German production of coal and steel as a whole under a common higher authority, within the framework of an organization open to the participation of other countries of Europe. The pooling of coal and steel production should immediately provide for the setting up of common foundations for economic development as a first step in the federation of Europe, and will change the destinies of those regions which have long been devoted to the manufacture of munitions of war, of which they have been the most constant victims. . . .
>
> Europe with new means at her disposal, will be able to pursue the realization of one of her essential tasks, the development of the African continent. . . .
>
> By pooling basic production and by instituting a new higher authority, whose decisions will bind France, Germany and other member countries, these proposals will bind the first concrete foundation of the European federation which is indispensable to the preservation of peace.[1]

The Schuman proposals won warm support from the supporters of European union. They received a less favourable reaction in the first instance from the producers of coal and steel, who were alarmed about the competition which they would face from across their borders. But they had little time to organize opposition or to counter the strong support for the proposal in Italy, Belgium, Luxembourg, and, to a lesser extent, Holland. It was these countries, together with France and Germany, which were to sign the treaty of the Coal and Steel Community and become the "Six" of Western Europe.

Outside those six countries Europe's two greatest producers of coal and steel were Sweden and Britain. It was unlikely that

[1] Royal Institute of International Affairs. *Documents, 1949–50*, pp. 315–16.

Sweden would take up the French proposals. It was traditionally neutral, its industry was geographically separate from the complex of continental Europe and it had shown no enthusiasm for the cause of European union. For Britain on the other hand the Schuman proposals represented a decisive moment of choice. In later years it became increasingly evident that the whole course of Britain's relations with Europe was affected by the decision it took in response to the Schuman Plan.

The Labour government declined to enter into negotiations with the French in response to their proposals of 9 May. It was consistent with all that the Labour government had said and done in relation to Europe that it should so decline. Defending its actions in the House of Commons Ernest Bevin pointed out that the terms on which Britain was invited to enter were the acceptance of the principle of supranationality in advance. Such an undertaking the British government was unable to give. In response the Conservatives strongly criticized the government's decision. They argued that the Dutch government had devised a formula which allowed Holland to join the discussions while keeping open the possibility of withdrawal. Should excessive demands be made Britain could similarly participate in discussions and influence their direction rather than abstaining from the start. It was of vital importance that the British government should so act because, as Eden argued in the House of Commons, it would be disastrous for Europe if the Schuman Plan did not succeed and disastrous for Britain if it succeeded without her.

The Labour government's case was weakened by the fact that it published a White Paper of its correspondence with the French on the same day that the Labour party published a pamphlet on European union. The pamphlet only represented in part the views of the Labour government. It rehearsed old Labour arguments against Britain joining a European union, in particular expressing strong suspicion of European conservatism and arguing that a British Labour government could only join a European union if it was sure that it would be based on Socialist parties. Although arguments of this sort discredited the government's case there can be little doubt that it was justified in supposing that supranationality was indeed a condition of participation in the Schuman Plan. The French government made it a condition because of its anxiety about German production, while the Federalists in Europe were at the height of their power in view of the disappointments over the Council of Europe and especially Britain's role in it. It was no more than realistic, therefore, for the British government to pose the issue in this way. What was open to question was not whether supranationality was an essential condition; but rather whether the degree of supranationality embodied in the Schuman proposals was in any way a serious threat to Britain in the immediate present and whether it was not, rather, a small price to pay for British participation in the long-term venture of European union. However that may be the British government declined the opportunity offered to it because it was not prepared to accept supranationality, and in so doing it undoubtedly represented the majority opinion in the country.

Six weeks after the Schuman proposals had been made events in Europe were given a new turn by the outbreak of war in Asia. Early in the morning on 25 June, North Korean troops crossed the thirty-eighth parallel and advanced on the South Korean capital of Seoul. The opening of armed hostility in this manner inevitably caused a crisis of first magnitude round the world. Korea had been ruled by the Japanese since the end of the nineteenth century. It had been one of the agreed objectives of the wartime allies to restore Korean independence once Japan was defeated. In practice this had proved impossible in any real sense. As Japan collapsed in August 1945 Russian troops accepted the surrender of the Japanese in North Korea and Americans in the south. Thereafter they had been unable to agree on a procedure whereby an independent government could be established over the whole of Korea. The Russians established a Communist government in the north, resisted all proposals for free elections, and refused to admit United Nations observers. The United States therefore provided the machinery for as free government as possible in the south and a United Nations commission supervised South Korean elections. In 1949 Russian and American troops were withdrawn, leaving in the south only an American military mission. The effect of this withdrawal was, however, to leave the North Koreans in a position of dominance as their army had been made bigger and more heavily equipped by the Russians.

The attack from the north in June 1950 was met with an immediate response by the United States and the United Nations. The Communists claimed that the war had begun as a result of an attack from the south, but their reports received little credence, the more so since the United Nations commission was still present in South Korea and could report directly to its parent body. President Truman had no hesitation in interpreting the attack as similar to the sort of aggression which had characterized Hitler's expansion in Europe before 1939, and he regarded it therefore as a test both of the democracies' will to resist and the strength of the United Nations. He immediately issued orders which prepared United States forces for action and instructed the United States delegate to the United Nations to summon an immediate meeting of the Security Council.

By some miscalculation, which has never been fully explained, the Russian delegate was absent from the United Nations because his government had boycotted the organization in protest against the continued representation of China by the Nationalist government instead of the Communists. As a result the United Nations could act as its founders had intended. It called for an immediate cease fire and then instructed its members to assist the government of South Korea. In this way there began a war which lasted in its most intense form until the spring of 1951 and then continued sporadically until the conclusion of an armistice two years later. Having begun as a small-scale attack by North Korea it was enlarged in the first place by the participation of some sixteen members of the United Nations (although the United States provided 90 per cent of the military forces) and then by the intervention of Chinese troops, as United Nations forces advanced northwards towards the frontier with Manchuria. It is generally assumed that the Soviet government was responsible for the initiation of the war; but it did nothing to enlarge the conflict once it had started and did not, as the Chinese did, commit its own forces.

The impact of the Korean War on events in Europe is not difficult to explain. Although the scene of action had shifted to Asia it was regarded as a further and more overt move in Russian expansion. The tempo and violence of Soviet policy appeared to be increasing in stages from the Czech *coup d'état* to the Berlin blockade and now to armed aggression. Moreover, there was a close superficial similarity between Korea and Germany. In both cases the Western powers had intended that a unified independent government should be established; in both cases the actual outcome had been a line of partition dividing one half of the country from the other. In Korea the Soviet Union was seen to have initiated an attack without involving its own forces by equipping and supporting a satellite, and there seemed no obstacle to a similar course of action in Europe. The result was to give a new and increased urgency to plans for the re-armament of western Europe and at the same time to bring into immediate relief the problem of whether or not to rearm West Germany. Although the North Atlantic Treaty had been signed a year earlier there had been little time to carry out practical measures of defence and the intention to do so had had to compete with the needs of economic reconstruction. Moreover, the participation of the Germans in their own defence had been pushed into the background because of the understandable fears and anxieties about German militarism present both in Germany and amongst its former victors.

The need to establish a defence force in Europe reopened the question of European rather than national reconstruction. The destruction caused by the Second World War had provided an incentive to economic reconstruction on a European basis. Similarly it could now be argued that if the military forces of the western European countries were to be rebuilt the rebuilding should be done within a European framework. Once again it was Winston Churchill who took the initiative in proposing such a step. In the Consultative Assembly of the Council of Europe in August 1950 he thrust aside the statute of the Council which prohibited the Assembly from discussing matters of defence, and urged the creation of a European army. His proposal was immediately sent to one of the Assembly's commissions which reported favourably and proposed the creation of a European Minister of Defence.

The practical difficulties of implementing such a proposal were great. It is difficult to see how any government, especially that of Great Britain, would have implemented Churchill's suggestion—even after Churchill became Prime Minister at the end of the following year. The question was still further complicated in September 1950 when the United States proposed to its major European allies that German rearmament was an indispensable prerequisite to the rearmament of western Europe. The proposal was first made to the foreign secretaries of France and Britain before the meeting of the NATO Council in New York. The United States government, as the provider of the material means of defence in Europe, and having its troops stationed there, was in a position to bring strong pressure on its allies. At the same time it provided an incentive by linking its proposal to an offer to provide an American Supreme Commander for NATO forces in Europe, thus reaffirming unmistakably its commitment to defence across the Atlantic.

Ernest Bevin, as British Foreign Secretary, was prepared to accept the American proposal. It offered the essential element to which he attached most importance—the participation of the United States in the defence and reconstruction of Europe. He was aware of the opposition which any suggestion of German rearmament aroused in Britain, and especially in his own party; but he believed he could survive such opposition. In contrast the French Foreign Minister, Schuman, was the representative of a country which had three times been invaded by German armies, and of a government which lacked the authority and party discipline of its British counterpart. He could give no promise that the French Assembly or people would accept German rearmament, and asked for time to seek a solution to the problem thus posed.

As the American proposal had followed the recommendation of the Council of Europe for the creation of a European army the obvious solution was to provide for the inclusion of German troops in a European army—to rearm Germans without creating a German army. The French government, which had already been so fertile in initiating the Schuman Plan, now turned to devising a similar solution to the problem of defence. Its first attempt took the form of a plan, named after René Pleven, the Minister of Defence, which would create a mixed army in which national contingents, including the German, would be "lost" in a European force. On closer examination integration to this extent appeared impossible of achievement, given the difficulties of communication, standardization of equipment—even catering. Yet the principle of subordinating national units to an international staff survived; and above all there was to be created a supranational commission exercising authority over the whole defence force. As these discussions were going on at the same time as the planning of the European Coal and Steel Community, it was logical to frame a closely similar pattern for defence. This was, in fact, done, and a treaty framed establishing a European Defence Community.

The result was that by 1951 two specific projects for closer union now existed, similar in their basic structure but markedly different in every other respect. The European Coal and Steel Community was the result of careful thought and preparation, while the Defence Community was a hastily devised solution to an emergency that had arisen unexpectedly as a result of the Korean War. The Coal and Steel Community proposed the establishment of a supranational authority over a sector of the political economy where the need for integration was most evident and the potential reward most obvious. Even so it had, as we have seen, excited the anxiety of producers faced with increased competition. The Defence Community in contrast proposed the abandonment of national sovereignty over the institution which for so many people is the very centre of nationalist feeling—the army—and required the surrender by national governments of control over their own national security. In short, it may be said that any protagonist of European union looking for the most ideal starting point for integration would have chosen the industrial complex of the Rhine and Moselle valleys, while any international saboteur of union would have suggested beginning with something as sensitive as national defence. This being so, it is not surprising that in the next few years the Coal and Steel Community established itself as a successful political and economic institution. The treaty establishing it was signed and ratified by the Six, and came into force in July 1952. The European Defence Community in contrast languished and died. The EDC Treaty was signed, but the French government repeatedly delayed seeking ratification by the parliament, until in 1954 it was finally rejected. Its rejection threatened the whole momentum of the European movement.

# CHAPTER 4

# Steel Succeeds while Defence Falters

THE purpose of the European Coal and Steel Community—ECSC —was to eliminate political barriers to the reconstruction and development of the coal and steel industry, and to remove the regulations and discriminations enacted by national governments which broke up a natural economic area. The institutions which it set up to this end represented a new departure in international organization. There already existed, in NATO and OEEC, a degree of co-operation and exchange of information between governments which was unprecedented. But their decisions were arrived at by representatives of national governments agreeing together, none of them being overruled by the others.

ECSC in contrast came under the direction of a supranational authority. The treaty establishing the Community gave power to a High Authority, and explicitly referred to its supranational character. The treaty stated:

> The members of the High Authority shall exercise their functions in complete independence in the general interests of the Community. In the fulfilment of their duties, they shall neither solicit nor accept instructions from any Government or any organization. They will abstain from all conduct incompatible with the supra-national character of their functions.
>
> Each Member State undertakes to respect this supra-national character and not to seek to influence the members of the High Authority in their decisions.

The implications of this part of the treaty are obvious. The High Authority had the responsibility of furthering the interests of the Community even when they ran counter to the interests of independent members as they might well in the short run. Under the treaty the High Authority was given the power to make appropriate regulations giving detailed application to the treaty and could levy tax to finance its operations.

At the same time the High Authority was made responsible to an Assembly of the Community. It was to report to the Assembly, and the Assembly could bring about its resignation by a vote of censure. In some ways this responsibility was similar to the responsibility of a national government to a parliament; but the Assembly of the Community was elected by national parliaments, and was not drawn directly from the electorate. Subsequently the development of other European institutions—the Common Market and the Atomic Energy Community—brought the establishment of two additional assemblies, which were then merged into a single assembly for all three communities, and given the title of European Parliament.

It was thus the intention of the treaty that the High Authority should be independent of national governments and of industrial interests—its members were not allowed to "exercise any business or professional activities related to coal and steel".

In spite of the advantages to be gained from ECSC, it is inconceivable that national governments would sign away their authority to a supranational body unless it were limited and controlled in some way. Moreover, within national systems of government the executive branch—to which the High Authority may be compared—is subject to the control of an Assembly and the check of a judicial system. It is understandable, therefore, that the High Authority should be subject to limitation and control. The scope of its action was in any case restricted to the area of the Community's responsibility—namely to the coal and steel industries and to the implementation of the treaty. In addition it was buttressed by other institutions enabling national governments to exercise a degree of control, permitting the expression of opinion, and ensuring the just application of rules and regulations.

Side by side with the High Authority the treaty established a Council of Ministers and defined carefully the relationship between the two. The High Authority could not proceed on matters of vital national concern without the approval of member governments as expressed in the Council of Ministers—while within its own sphere the High Authority retained its supranational character independent of the Council. The Council consisted of one representative from each government.

The dividing line between matters which fell within the competence of the Authority and those over which national governments claim the deciding voice could not be drawn once for all. In general terms it was the responsibility of the Council to "harmonize the action of the High Authority with that of the governments which are responsible for the general economic policy of their countries". Even the implementation of more specific terms of the treaty depended on political circumstances, on the outlook of governments —and on the pressures to which governments themselves are subjected by groups directly affected by the regulation of industry. In consequence the successful working of the Community depended on a sensitive assessment by the High Authority of the reactions of member governments. Its success in the early years followed from its ability to judge political circumstances with accuracy.

This was the more important because its task went beyond the mere removal of tariff barriers. Even when *laissez-faire* ideas predominated in nineteenth-century England industry was subject to government regulation. (Travellers on the early railways in Britain enjoyed the convenience of the "Parliamentary"—a train service which the companies were required to provide, under act of Parliament, at a penny a mile.) In addition to removing tariff barriers the Community was therefore faced with the need to secure uniformity in the regulations governing the production, transport, and marketing of the products under its charge. In its own sphere it would act always in consultation with national governments as well as representatives of industry. It is a common experience of governments in the regulation and control of industry that they must consult with interested parties, producers, trade unions, and, as far as possible, consumers, if their rules and regulations are to take practical effect. The experience of the High Authority was to be the same, with the additional complexity that for them national governments were amongst the interested parties whose views they had to take into account.

The first part of the Community's plan was achieved quickly and smoothly. The treaty itself required the abandonment of tariffs and quotas between the members and this requirement was carried out. Tariffs and quotas were in any case few in both coal and iron ore. A more complicated question immediately arose in the matter of transport rates. The cost of transporting the weighty commodities of the coal and steel industry is obviously a major part of their cost to producers. Transport rates had been subject to national regulations based on a variety of considerations, such as the desire to help a particular region, or to assist rail transport in competition with water or for strategic purposes. The result was that the cost of transporting an identical load could vary substantially according to the national area it crossed. If a genuine Common Market were to be created such discrepancies as this had to be removed and one of the major early tasks of the Community was to move a long way in this direction. In doing so it had constantly to seek out compromises and agreements with national governments since the changes which Community policy required affected the whole structure of national transport rates.

At the same time the High Authority was taking over some of the functions of national governments with the intention of framing a policy to the advantage of the Community as a whole. A prominent example of this was its activity in relation to scrap steel. The steel industry in the Community area depended on supplies of scrap to maintain an adequate production of finished steel, but a large proportion of scrap had to be imported from the United States. The import of scrap would in any case have been the subject of governmental intervention since it involved the expenditure of foreign exchange and competition with domestic pig-iron industry. The difference which resulted from the institution of the Community was that this intervention ceased to be the concern of governments alone and was taken over by the High Authority, in consultation with governments, in an attempt to ensure that the whole area enjoyed the same advantages. The task was complicated by differences in the strength of the national pig-iron industries and the varying suitability of different steel-making processes to the use of scrap.

Complicated as these tasks were, considerable success attended the High Authority's efforts in dealing with them. This was so in part because the production of iron and steel rose throughout the early years of the Community's life, as did the demand for iron and steel products. The adjustments which were made were therefore easier to carry out. Individual producers who suffered from the removal of a particular advantage or an element of protection (for example, differential transport rates) received some compensation from the growth of the economy and of the aggregate demand for their products. Whether production would have increased equally without the institution of the Community is impossible to say; there is no doubt that growth was in large part due to natural causes outside the Community's control. It is certain, however, that trade within the Community did increase and there were specific examples of a growth in trade between particular areas with a natural economic link which previously had been kept apart by differences of national regulation.

The story of coal production was less encouraging. Here too the Community took over governmental functions in arranging for the transfer of miners from outworn coal fields to those that were more prosperous. This was done, for example, in the removal of miners with their families and household effects from the Loire area of France to the north-east of the country. But whereas the demand for iron and steel went on increasing, coal found itself subject to competition in the late 1950's from new sources of power, particularly oil. Coal was thereby rendered less profitable and a wise economic policy called for the closing of uneconomic pits. In this area the Community was on the whole less successful in its negotiations with national governments since the latter had to bear the direct political impact of such closures from which the institutions of the Community were sheltered.

The early success of the Coal and Steel Community contrasted sharply with the false start made in the field of defence, as the EDC treaty encountered growing opposition. In Italy it was naturally opposed by the Communist party, which continued to hold some 25 per cent of the electoral vote, and by the Socialists. But the Christian Democratic party, as the strongest single party, retained a strong hold on Parliament and had every incentive to support the treaty. The Christian Democratic government favoured European union for its own sake and welcomed an arrangement for defence which would give equality to Italy without imposing excessive burdens. The Benelux countries for their part were too small to entertain seriously an independent defence policy and too recently acquainted with their own vulnerability to attack to seek an escape into neutrality.

It was in Germany and France that opposition was strongest. We have already seen that in Germany there was strong opposition to the European policy of Adenauer, since it appeared to sacrifice the possibility of German reunification. This body of opinion was strengthened when the sensitive issue of defence was brought to the forefront of the European question. Moreover, in spite of the fears felt and expressed outside Germany that German rearmament would bring a rebirth of German militarism, the German people showed considerable reluctance to rearm. In the second of the great wars of which Germany had been the centre the German armies had suffered devastating casualties on the eastern front and the German homeland had been subjected to massive bombardment and then to occupation. This experience, rather than the re-education which the occupying powers had stressed as part of their occupation policy, had done much to remove old-fashioned German militarism.

The Soviet government was well aware of feeling in West Germany and sought vigorously to prevent ratification of the EDC Treaty by holding out the promise of possible German reunification. As a result of its initiative a conference of the foreign ministers of the four occupying powers was held in the spring and early summer of

1951 to explore the possibility of a German settlement—but without result. Nonetheless the government of East Germany as well as the Soviet government kept up a barrage of pronouncements and notes inviting their Western counterparts to agree to a German peace treaty and German reunification. The most striking of these was a Soviet note of 10 March 1952—the anniversary of a speech by Stalin in 1939 which later proved part of the prelude to the Nazi–Soviet pact. The note was distinctive in that it suggested the possibility of German reunification without insisting on German disarmament. It excluded German membership of alliances, but it accepted that Germany should have its own national army on a limited scale.

Neither the Adenauer government nor any of the three Western occupying powers was prepared to regard the note of 10 March as providing a significant opportunity for negotiations with the Russians. They insisted that the only satisfactory basis for German reunification, desirable as this was in itself, was the holding of free elections throughout Germany. To this Stalin would never give his consent. They therefore interpreted the overtures coming from the East as designed to thwart progress towards ratification of the EDC Treaty.

Nonetheless, Russian initiatives received a favourable response from sections of West German opinion, particularly from the Social Democratic party whose leaders believed that the note of 10 March was at least a favourable opening which should have been explored. They therefore used every opportunity to attack the government and they tried to prevent acceptance of the EDC Treaty by bringing a case before the Constitutional Court on the grounds that rearmament was unconstitutional. All their efforts were, however, unsuccessful. The Constitutional Court declined to pronounce on an issue which was not yet the subject of a law. More important, when elections were held in September 1953 the Christian Democrats won an outstanding victory such that in alliance with two other smaller parties they could command the two-thirds majority necessary for constitutional revision, thus cutting through the knot of the constitutionality of rearmament.

In this way the distrust which a majority of the people of Western

Germany felt of the Soviet Union and its intentions, coupled with the success of the Adenauer government in restoring the economic prosperity of the country, overruled the strong opposition to re-armament even though there was so little enthusiasm for a return to uniforms and military service. By March 1954 both houses of the German legislature had ratified the EDC treaty, it had also been ratified in Belgium, Holland, and Luxemburg, while in Italy the completion of ratification was only a matter of time.

It was therefore in France that the issue remained to be decided and there events ran in the opposite direction to Germany. France, like Italy, had a very strong Communist party—in 1946 it was the largest single party in the National Assembly. Fresh elections were held in June 1951 and although the popular Communist vote did not alter significantly—it was approximately 23 per cent of the votes cast—the number of Communist deputies in the Assembly was reduced from 180 to 100 by a device incorporated in the new elec-toral law. This reduction of Communist strength in the Assembly was, however, outweighed by the emergence at these elections of a strong body—some 120—of Gaullist deputies belonging to the Rally of the French People which de Gaulle had started in 1947. The Gaullists (even though many former supporters of Vichy were now included in their following) had no illusions about the necessity of defence in the face of the Communist threat; but their concern was with *national* defence, and they were opposed to any sacrifice of French sovereignty by the absorption of the French army into a European Community.

The combination of Communist and Gaullist votes in the Assembly made it extremely difficult to secure a majority for ratifi-cation of the EDC treaty. Moreover, even amongst the centre parties, particularly the Radicals and the Socialists, the proposed arrangements excited little enthusiasm and some opposition. This was the more so as the threat of attack appeared less imminent and the general level of tension in international relations diminished. The war in Korea was very much reduced in scale after 1951, even though it took until 1953 for an armistice to be concluded. In October 1952 the Nineteenth Congress of the Communist Party of the Soviet Union was held and the speeches made there, particularly by Malenkov, were interpreted as indicating a withdrawal by the Soviet Union from the forward policies which had characterized recent years. In March 1953 Stalin died and many people, including Winston Churchill, thought this provided a possible opportunity for fresh discussions with the Russians. In June of the same year riots in East Berlin and elsewhere in East Germany brought Soviet tanks on to the streets in such a way as to render suspect Russian statements of their intention towards Germany. But the riots also had the effect of increasing anxiety in the West about the dangers of rearming West Germany since they seemed to open up the possibility of a war in Europe caused by an East German uprising supported by armed force from West Germany. In this way, while the necessity for extreme measures of defence against the Soviet Union seemed less, the dangers of rearming Germany appeared greater.

The French attitude to the European Defence Community may well have been different had British policy towards European union changed significantly. Many people expected that it would do so when a Conservative government took office in November 1951. Winston Churchill, the great initiator and leader of the European movement, was once again Prime Minister, supported in his government by men like Macmillan, Duncan Sandys, and Maxwell Fyfe, who had been in the forefront of the Council of Europe.

But as we have seen, these men, enthusiastic as they were about the general cause of European union, had never been in favour of any surrender of British sovereignty. Their argument had always been that if Britain were to participate in the European movement it could help shape European unity along lines acceptable to itself. When they took office this was no longer possible. The Federal current was in full flood in Europe and the choice open to the Conservative government was between full membership of the Coal and Steel Community and the Defence Community, or a weak association with the European institutions. Nothing had happened to make the government willing to join the Coal and Steel Community in its existing form. The iron and steel industry itself was relieved to escape from nationalization (to which it would have been subjected if the Labour government's legislation were not repealed by its Conservative successor) and it had no wish to be subordinated to the European authority. Nor was the incentive to join the Defence Community any greater. The imperative need was to provide for actual defence forces in Europe, and the British government was relieved to discover that it had American support in trying to create such a force without adding to the existing complications of integrating Britain into a Defence Community.

The outcome was that the British government set about negotiating a Treaty of Association with the Coal and Steel Community. A British mission was attached to the High Authority as soon as the Coal and Steel Community was established and a formal agreement concluded in December 1954. In this way communication was established between Britain and the Community but the British representative at Luxembourg, where the High Authority was established, naturally did not enter into the decisions of the Community. At the same time Anthony Eden, as Foreign Minister, suggested that the Coal and Steel Community and the Defence Community should both be answerable in some way and should report to the Council of Europe so as to provide a means of associating the Six with the other members of the Council of Europe. However his plan received a cold welcome and had no practical outcome.

In defence matters both Britain and the United States signed a series of guarantees to the EDC powers in the hope of encouraging the French to ratify the EDC treaty and allaying the various anxieties which existed about the rearmament of Germany. The most extensive of the guarantees which the two countries offered came in the spring of 1954 when the British undertook to appoint a representative to attend meetings of the Council of Ministers of the Defence Community and to maintain forces on the continent of Europe, part of which would be included in European formations. The United States similarly undertook to retain armed forces in Europe to consult with the European Defence Community about the level and deployment of its forces.

Meanwhile, on the continent of Europe, the Federalists were looking ahead to the time when EDC would be ratified, and had already devised a plan for a European Political Community which would go a step further in the establishment of European federal institutions. These proposals were embodied in a draft treaty in March 1953, providing amongst other things for the establishment of a European Parliament elected by universal suffrage. Until the EDC Treaty was ratified, however, it was useless to attempt any further movement towards a political community.

By this time the American government was growing increasingly impatient with the delays over EDC and the consequent obstacle to the strengthening of European defence. In the United States too there had been a change of government—at the end of 1952 the Democrats lost the presidential election for the first time since 1932 and President Eisenhower took office in January 1953, appointing John Foster Dulles as his Secretary of State. Initially the American government had not favoured the EDC project, which it regarded as a complicated way of providing for a German contribution to the defence of Europe. Once the European nations, however, had taken up the EDC idea it was intent on bringing the project to a speedy realization. In consequence the new administration, especially Dulles as Secretary of State, was increasingly impatient with the French, whose prestige through 1953 and 1954 diminished rapidly. It was at this time that the faults of French government seemed most obvious —a multiplicity of parties produced either a quick succession of coalitions, or complete inaction as the price of government stability. In Indo-China the French were fighting a war which was supported financially by the United States but in which they seemed unable to achieve either military victory or political progress—instead their conduct of the war was discredited by scandals of a sort all too familiar in recent French history.

Impatient and distrustful of France, Dulles was impressed in contrast with the record of success of Adenauer in West Germany. At no point had Adenauer wavered in his support for Western unity and Western defence, and he had succeeded in overcoming his critics and opponents. It seemed poor reward for the West Germans, therefore, that because of the delay in the ratification of EDC, the next step in the establishment of German sovereignty should be delayed. Britain, France, and the United States were ready to end their occupation of Western Germany and to sign a new treaty giving the German government control over its own affairs, provided that it still allowed stationing of Western troops on its territory—but the implementation of such an agreement was held up until the question of the German army was settled. Should France continue to be a weak partner in the Western system, therefore, there was an obvious incentive for the United States to alter the pivot of its European policy and centre it on the Germany of Adenauer—the more so since Dulles's personal connections with Europe happened to be with Germany more than any other country.

It was these considerations that lay behind the pressure which Dulles brought for the ratification of the EDC treaty. Up to this time the American government had always been chary of bringing pressure on its European allies, aware of the danger that they would react in the opposite direction. In 1953 Dulles abandoned the restraint of his predecessors and made a public speech in which he said:

> The United States is primarily concerned that European civilization should survive and prosper. Our concern has been demonstrated through . . . vast material contributions for economic aid, and the stationing in Europe of substantial ground and air forces, with strong naval support. . . . But decisive steps remain to be taken. . . . Mere promises for the future are not enough to bury a past replete with bitter memories. . . . If however the European Defence Community should not become effective; if France and Germany remain apart, so that they would again be potential enemies, then indeed there would be grave doubt whether Continental Europe could be made a place of safety. That would compel an agonizing reappraisal of basic United States policy.[1]

Not surprisingly his speech scarcely had the effect he intended; instead it was an important contribution to the resentment which already existed in France towards the power and the policies of the United States.

The sequence of events came to a climax in the summer of 1954.

[1] *New York Times*, 15 December 1953.

At that time there was a change of government in France and Pierre Mendès France became Prime Minister. He was faced with an imminent military crisis in Indo-China and he took over negotiations already started at a foreign ministers' conference in Geneva for a political settlement in that country. This was his most urgent task and he undertook to reach a settlement within twenty-one days or to resign. But he also intended to settle the question of the Defence Community. He had never been a supporter of European federalism and in any case he recognized the need for a vote to be taken on EDC so that if, as he believed, no majority could be found for it, a fresh start could be made. He succeeded in meeting his undertaking with regard to Indo-China, and the war was brought to an end with the division of Vietnam into north and south—albeit a temporary respite in the conflict that tore that country asunder. This done he sought to modify the EDC treaty to meet the objections brought against it in his own country: but without success. On 30 August a vote was carried in the National Assembly rejecting the EDC treaty.

The immediate consequences for the defence of western Europe were not important. As we have seen, the danger of a Russian attack in Europe, as distinct from encroachment on the Western position in Berlin, had certainly been exaggerated. Such danger did not exist during the period of confusion in the Russian leadership following the death of Stalin. But the political repercussions threatened to be immense. It was not possible to turn the clock back to the days before the German army and the European Defence Community had first been proposed. Some means had to be found of giving West Germany its sovereignty and an alternative to EDC regulating German rearmament had therefore to be found. Moreover, the collapse of EDC threatened to undermine the whole movement towards European union. The next step had been delayed pending the ratification of the EDC treaty and it looked now as if the next step might never be taken. Only those with strong belief in the future of European union could foresee at this time that within a few years the trend to federalism would emerge stronger than ever.

The gap created by the rejection of EDC in the politics of defence in Europe provided one of the few occasions when British intervention in European questions could be decisive—although as we shall see it was less so than when Bevin took up the Marshall offer. Somehow a means had to be found to permit German rearmament as a part of the restoration of German sovereignty without taking on the full commitment of supranationality and without running the risks of an excessively strong German military force.

In meeting this problem Anthony Eden found fresh inspiration, if we are to believe his memoirs, as he sat in his bath. The Brussels Treaty had provided machinery and institutions for the defence of western Europe. It had been devised when Germany and Italy were still thought of as former enemies, but it appeared to Eden that its central provisions, particularly the establishment of a Consultative Council, could be reshaped to meet the present needs. He therefore set out on a tour of the capitals of western Europe to seek support for his ideas. His journey crossed with that of Dulles, who (without informing Eden) had decided to visit western Europe too—although he rather pointedly left out Paris from his itinerary. Relations between Eden and Dulles were already rather strained at this time. Eden had taken the unusual step of advising Eisenhower against the appointment of Dulles as Secretary of State when Eisenhower was elected President. Now, in 1954, they had differed widely over policy in South-east Asia, Dulles refusing to sign the Geneva agreements of which Eden was a principal architect. Dulles also reproached Britain for its coolness towards EDC. We may presume, however, that Dulles's mission to Europe made clear to him that there was no possibility of reviving EDC and he left the initiative in diplomacy therefore to Eden.

Finding sufficient support for his ideas Eden proceeded with the organization of a conference to be attended by the western European governments together with Canada and the United States. When the conference met at the end of September 1954 it was able to reach agreement on the establishment of a new organization which was substantially an enlargement and reconstruction of the Brussels Treaty Organization, renamed Western European Union. The membership of the WEU was to be the six EDC countries together with Britain. The most important institution of the new organization was to be a Council of Ministers and to this was added an Assembly which would meet annually to review decisions by the Council of Ministers. At the same time the treaty establishing WEU included provisions to meet certain specific needs as they were seen at that time. The German contribution was limited in size, and as Germany undertook to keep no armed forces outside the Union this constituted an effective maximum limit on German rearmament. Germany also undertook not to manufacture "A, B, C" weapons—that is for atomic, bacteriological, or chemical warfare. The British government at the same time undertook to keep a minimum level of forces on the mainland of Europe—four divisions and the second tactical airforce. The British government undertook not to withdraw these forces without the consent of the majority of the members of the WEU, except in an acute overseas emergency. Germany was to be admitted to NATO and it was agreed that all armed forces in Europe should come under the authority of the NATO Supreme Commander. In this way the existing members of NATO having overseas forces retained independent sovereign control over them but, in common with Germany, they placed their forces on the continent of Europe under NATO command.

In the long run the careful construction of WEU with its special provisions at one and the same time to restrict the size of the German army and keep up the size of the British forces in Europe was of little practical importance. WEU was of most importance in permitting German rearmament after the defeat of EDC and in smoothing the way of Germany into membership of NATO. Once this had been done military planning and intergovernmental co-operation was achieved through NATO. Although the WEU Council and Assembly met as intended, they did not have a great influence on the course of events. Within a few years of the WEU agreement, the British government decided to reduce its forces on the continent and secured the consent of WEU to do so—but in circumstances which left little effective choice to Britain's partners in Europe.

The settlement of the defence question made it possible to proceed with an agreement between Britain, France, the United States, and Germany for the establishment of the German Federal Republic as a fully sovereign power, which accepted the limitations of the WEU agreement and agreed to the stationing of troops on its territory. This important landmark in the history of western Europe was not passed without further hesitation and doubt on the part of the French parliament. Indeed when the agreements concerning Germany came before the French Council of the Republic (the French second chamber) they were at first rejected, so that a procedural device had to be used to secure a second vote by which they were ratified. The WEU agreement was not open to the objections of those who feared supranationality. The fundamental reason for its acceptance was the realization that its rejection would result in the diplomatic isolation of France and the possible establishment of a Washington–Bonn axis detrimental to French interests.

One apparently small issue remained to be settled in the relations between Germany and France. This was the question of the Saar—a small area on the border between the two countries rich in coal and iron and consequently a subject of dispute between them in their recent history. After the First World War the Saar had been placed under League of Nations control until a plebiscite (under the terms of the Treaty of Versailles) returned it to Germany in 1935. After the Second World War it fell within the French zone of occupation, but from an early date the French government established a special regime for the Saar by which it became politically autonomous and economically integrated with France. In this way the French derived maximum benefit from the coal and steel industry in the Saar and the Saarlanders were content as long as their position was so much better than that of the Germans. These conditions changed as the West German economy recovered and the establishment of a West German government made it possible for Adenauer and his colleagues to state their own claims with regard to the Saar.

When this happened the Saar territory once again became an important irritant in Franco–German relations. Those in France and Germany who most wanted Franco–German co-operation in a

European framework nonetheless found themselves taking conflict-ing views about the Saar, while their critics exploited Franco–German differences to attack their European policy. Adenauer in particular was repeatedly challenged by those who opposed his policy of European union on the grounds that he was surrendering German interests in the Saar.

Outside France and Germany the obvious solution to the Saar question seemed to be to use the new institutions and the new atmosphere in Europe to provide a novel regime for the Saar. A plan was drawn up, named after its principal author, Van Naters, which placed the Saar under a European authority. When France and Germany reached agreement on defence and German sover-eignty in 1954 they also agreed on a Saar statute, based on the Van Naters plan, to be submitted to a referendum by the Saarlanders. It appeared that the Saar question would be liquidated at the same time as West Germany achieved its own sovereignty. In the event this proved not to be the case. The Saarlanders were not confident enough in the future of Europe to accept the unusual solution pro-posed for them and therefore rejected the Saar statute when the referendum took place in October 1955.

No alternative possibility had been offered to them, but by this time it was obvious to the French government that the Saarlanders wished to return to Germany and would never be persuaded that the Saar was properly part of France. They therefore opened fresh discussions with Germany which resulted in an agreement for the restitution of the Saar to Germany. At the same time the two countries reached an agreement of great practical importance pro-viding for the canalization of the Moselle river, to be paid for in part by the Germans. The incorporation of the Saar into Germany took place on 1 January 1957 and after a slightly longer period the Moselle river, beautiful and productive of wine as it had always been, became a great waterway linking French industry to the Rhine.

Before this had happened a fresh start had been made in the move-ment towards closer integration in western Europe.

# CHAPTER 5

# Nationalism and Communism in Eastern Europe

IN THE ten years which followed the end of the war, western Europe made great strides forward towards closer integration, in spite of the rejection of the EDC Treaty. Initially this development occurred with the support of the United States and with American participation in NATO and OEEC. The United States gave an important lead and took the initiative, and Americans experienced no difficulty in seeing European integration as a response to American commitment to Europe.

East of the line which divided Europe conditions were very different. In the Communist world there had long existed a degree and kind of unity which the non-Communist world had never known. In the years immediately following the Russian Revolution in 1917 the Russian Communists had established their control over Communist parties in other countries, and started new parties wherever possible. In countries like France and Italy the labour movement was divided into those who followed Moscow and those who wished to retain their independent status and follow a less revolutionary form of socialism. In Great Britain, where the Labour party was able to mobilize the most important part of the labour movement, the Russians sent emissaries and money to start a Communist party.

The advantage the Russian leaders enjoyed was that they could use the power of the Russian state to dominate Communist parties in other countries. In countries like France and Britain there were small parties without any position in the government. Elsewhere they were declared illegal and suppressed. Russia—the Union of Soviet Socialist Republics—enjoyed great prestige because it was the one and only country where the Communist movement had been successful in a revolution and had taken over the state. Since Communist ideology believed in an inevitable historical development towards a Communist society, the one Communist party which had made immense progress in this direction was assured of great respect and authority. It could claim to be right because it had been successful. Its prestige was further enhanced when it survived the Second World War and showed that a Communist society could resist the attacks of a powerful enemy.

As well as prestige the Russians had power and money. Their secret police and agents could travel abroad and control the development of other Communist parties. If they wished to eliminate a foreign Communist they could do so by their own methods, or by denouncing him to the police; or they could make sure that the supply of funds went to his rival.

In this way the international Communist movement was welded into an exceptionally well-disciplined international organization. A formal body, the Communist International or Comintern, had been founded in 1919 and national Communist parties were supposed to take part in its deliberations and the formulation of Communist policies. Instead the Comintern came to be one of the means by which Moscow transmitted instructions to other parties—whether secretly, or at its congresses. The Russians also used its chain of command to enforce their decisions. In this way the Russian government, under Stalin, was able to bring about rapid changes of policy, which were followed by national Communist parties, whether or not it suited their own advantage.

The advent of the war in 1939 produced two such rapid changes of front in the Communist movement. From 1935 until 1939 Communist parties were strong supporters of rearmament, at a time when the Soviet Union was trying to mobilize the Western powers into a policy of resistance to Germany. But in August 1939 the Soviet Union succeeded in agreeing on a non-aggression pact with

Germany, in such a way that Germany attacked Poland while the Russians remained neutral and themselves occupied the eastern part of Poland. Communist parties in all countries had to follow this change of front. When Britain declared war because of the German attack on Poland the British Communists at first supported the government—and then had quickly to retract on instructions from Moscow. Soon afterwards the French Communists were being told not to support a policy of resistance to Germany when France fell; they therefore denounced de Gaulle and the Free French as continuing the fight only for financial and stock-exchange interests. But in June 1941 Germany attacked Russia; then the French Communists, and all others, had to switch to support for the war against Germany.

As far as he was able, Stalin kept his control of foreign Communists in being during the war. In some cases the task was easier, because an important group of Communists fled to Moscow when their own countries were overrun. But in 1943 he dissolved the formal apparatus of the Comintern. His full reasons for doing so are not known; but it suited Russian foreign policy at the time, because it mollified the suspicions of the Western powers with which Russia was now in alliance against Germany.

With the end of the war the Russian army spread across eastern Europe and in one country after another Communist governments were brought into power over a period of two and a half years—culminating in the Czech *coup d'état* in February 1948. These governments depended on the Russians to maintain themselves in power. Except in Czechoslovakia it was the Russian army which provided the final coercive force in case of trouble—and possibly the army would have been used in Czechoslovakia if necessary. Because they were dependent on the Russians, and because of the practice which had been built up before the war, Stalin was able to direct them in the course of his choosing, and to determine who should participate in these new Communist governments.

No new institutional arrangements were necessary for this control to be maintained. True, a new institution was established in 1947, called the Communist Information Bureau, or Cominform; and another in 1949, the Council of Mutual Economic Assistance, or Comecon. But their role was a subsidiary one. The Cominform was not so extensive in its membership as its predecessor the Comintern —it only included the Communist parties of eastern Europe (except Albania) and those of France and Italy. It held meetings and published a journal with the lengthy title: *For a Lasting Peace, for a People's Democracy*, and these were useful and important channels of communication. Comecon was even less important during Stalin's life, although it was given a much larger role after he had died.

The control which the Russians exercised was therefore of a more direct kind—by bilateral arrangements with each country. Russian ambassadors were key men in the transmission of directives; the Russian secret police constructed national security forces and retained control over them. The system of purges which had developed before the war was maintained, so that the men who were put in key posts were Stalin's creatures and his men. Lifelong Communists who had played a major part in the east European Communist parties were imprisoned or executed—men like Gottwald in Poland, Rajk in Hungary, and Kostov in Bulgaria.

But there was one country which Stalin could not control—and that was Yugoslavia. In Yugoslavia alone of the eastern European states, communism had come to power without any assistance from the Russians, and as it did so it created a strong fusion between nationalism and communism.

Nationalism had always been a strong force in Yugoslavia—but it had usually been a divisive force. Small nations aroused loyalty and fanaticism, and divisions were especially deep between Serbs and Croats. All the major forces making for divisive nationalism seemed to be present in prewar Yugoslavia. Croats were Catholic while Serbs were Orthodox Christians; the Croats were proud of an ancient medieval kingdom, and of their place in the Roman Empire; the Serbs had fought in the First World War as an independent state and attached little importance to the Croats' historical pride. The Croats had wanted a Federal Yugoslavia, but found themselves dominated by the Serbs, and ruled dictatorially by a Serb king— while the Serbs retorted that the Croats could have had a larger part in the running of the state if they had not chosen a policy of obstructionism and non-co-operation.

The advent of the war did not end these rivalries, but the course of the fighting did much to change them. The German attack on Yugoslavia in the spring of 1941 occurred because the Yugoslavs were not prepared meekly to allow German troops to go through Yugoslavia to Greece, and threw out their own government in a popular revolt rather than do so. In the ensuing campaign the Communists, under the leadership of Josip Broz—Tito—were in an unusually strong position, since they had prepared, as a clandestine party, for an armed take-over of power before the war. In June 1941 their drive and determination increased, because the fatherland of communism—Russia—was attacked by Germany. They did not provide the only resistance force; on the contrary there was an important Partisan army led by General Mihailovitch, in association with the royal Yugoslav government in exile, which initially appeared from the outside as the best-organized force against the Germans. But Mihailovitch was a Serb, as were his followers, while the Communists succeeded in mobilizing men of all nations, subordinating national differences to their own Communist–Partisan ideology and using Communist skills in the organization of them. As a result the British government decided in the middle of the war that it should give what support it could to Tito rather than Mihailovitch, and supplies of material as well as advisers were flown in.

As a result the Yugoslav Partisans were never beaten, and the defeat of Germany meant that the Yugoslavs retained the independence for which they had fought so vigorously. Tito and his followers had not fought only for independence—they were also determined to change the old political and social order and instal a Communist government. In this they found themselves at odds with the Soviet government. As the war ended Stalin wanted to keep the grand alliance in being, and for this reason—possibly for other reasons too—was cautious in his promotion of Communist objectives, especially when they were not under his close control. He therefore tried to restrain the Yugoslavs from going too fast in establishing a Communist state; and he refused to support the claims which they made on the frontier area of Trieste.

A Yugoslav victory—with the help of the British but not the Russians—had thus produced intense national Communist emotion in Yugoslavia, coupled with an awareness of growing differences between Yugoslavia and Russia. As the post-war years proceeded, the Russians tried to extend the same controls over Yugoslavia as in other eastern European countries. The demands which the Russians imposed on the Yugoslavs were set out in correspondence between the Communist parties of the two countries—correspondence which was published in the West. Many of the arguments used were mere talking points—the degree of collectivization in agriculture, the structure of the Yugoslav Communist party and the way it governed the country. The key issues were those of control—the Russians wanted to have their own police in Yugoslavia—and of leadership. It had been normal practice in prewar days for Moscow to support one foreign Communist leader against another, and the Soviet–Yugoslav correspondence shows that the Russians were now backing an alternative Communist, named Hebrang, as a rival to Tito for the leadership. No doubt Hebrang would have been more amenable to Stalinist control. There were differences too over the role which Yugoslavia could expect to play in its traditional area of interest in the Balkans—which the Soviet government now dominated.

Tito and the Yugoslavs resisted the Russian demands. As a result there was a complete break between Soviet Russia and Yugoslavia in June 1948, and Yugoslavia was expelled from the Cominform. It was one of the most significant events of the postwar years.

Tito was able to refuse Stalin's demands because he controlled the power of a Communist state. He was no longer the struggling leader of a prewar party, dependent on the Russians for money and in constant danger of arrest and imprisonment. The resources of Yugoslavia appeared—and were—meagre in 1948. It was not a rich country, it was ravaged by war, its people had in some areas been kept alive by food sent by the United Nations. But it was an independent state, and short of invasion there was little the Russians could do—in the ensuing years every means of blockade and pressure was used to no effect. Tito commanded the apparatus of the state, and the loyalty of the majority of Yugoslavs. For the time being no other eastern European state had any firm base from which to resist the Russians, and none achieved the same independence as Yugoslavia. But as independent state structures were established and national loyalties re-emerged, independence grew stronger. The break with Yugoslavia revealed that Russian control of other Communists was placed in a totally different context once those Communists gained control of the state—as the Chinese were to do the following year.

The core of the Soviet–Yugoslav dispute had been over questions of power; but there were also divergent views of the way a Communist state should develop. The break with Russia confirmed the Yugoslav government in its view that it should devise its own Socialist policies. The Soviet Union had developed the Communist party and the police into the main instruments of totalitarian rule; the Yugoslavs believed that an essential part of a Socialist state was that the workers should participate in its direction. Within certain limitations this was achieved, and workers' councils were established with a share in the management of industrial enterprises. As the years went on greater liberalism appeared in Yugoslavia— although one of Tito's lieutenants, Milovan Djilas, was put in prison when he published a book entitled *The New Class*, criticizing the new Communist autocracy. In this way a new ideology began to emerge. No longer was the Soviet Union the sole interpreter of what Communist policy should be, the single oracle to translate Communist theory into day-to-day practice. Those who were discontent with Soviet Communist rule could look to Yugoslavia and see an alternative road to socialism. A national Communist state had thus come into existence. Paradoxically it was formed in the country most noted before the war for its divisive nationalisms. In the new state these did not disappear; but they were greatly weakened and subordinated to the overriding appeal of Yugoslav patriotism and independence.

Internationally, Yugoslavia was able to maintain its position. In great economic difficulty, it received aid from the Western powers. Careful negotiations even made it possible for the United States to give military assistance, in spite of Yugoslav attachment to their own independence and American fears about aid going to a Communist state. In 1953–4 Tito made the furthest move towards a Western position in international politics when Yugoslavia signed a Balkan alliance with Greece and Turkey—both NATO members. In the long term Yugoslav foreign policy was that of neutralism, and as an ever-growing number of African and Asian states gained their independence it came to play a leading role amongst them.

In 1948 the Yugoslav break with Russia was a single isolated act of defiance. Ten years later it can be seen as the beginning of a movement of major importance in eastern Europe. In March 1953 Stalin died, and the kingpin of the old Communist system was removed. It was inevitable that after such a long period of absolute rule there should be a struggle for power amongst the possible successors for some time afterwards, but by 1955 it was clear that Khrushchev was the dominant figure. To most of the new leaders it was obvious that the Stalinist system was in need of drastic renewal. Men who had grown up in the terror and tyranny of the police state—who had indeed commanded various levels of it in order to survive—were aware of the wastage of manpower it involved, and the hideous quality of life it produced. Internationally the foreign policy of the Soviet Union had been met by a strong Western alliance, and the rearmament of West Germany was virtually certain, whether or not the EDC treaty was ratified. In eastern Europe Yugoslavia had been thrust out from the Soviet bloc.

For whatever reasons, Stalin's successors made a vigorous effort to reshape Russian policies. Two outstanding conflicts in the Far East were liquidated—the obstacles to an armistice agreement in Korea at last disappeared so that an exchange of prisoners could be made and peace restored (without there being any final settlement). In Indo-China the war which the French had been fighting for seven years was halted. Indo-China was divided along the seventeenth parallel and arrangements made for the withdrawal of French troops. Molotov played a key role in the negotiation of the settlement—which left a Communist North Vietnam and an independent South Vietnam poised, as events turned out, for fresh conflict and fresh intervention in the years that followed.

In Europe the Soviet Union made two important withdrawals. It withdrew from the naval base which it had insisted the Finns should make available to it after the end of the Second World War. It withdrew its opposition to the conclusion of a peace treaty with Austria, so that Austria could be freed from the presence of occupation forces and take full advantage of its independence. The settlement required Austria to remain a neutral country—that is to say not to join NATO—but this requirement accorded well with Austrian policy. The Soviet Union insisted on payments being made in compensation for the German assets which it had claimed under the Potsdam Agreement and which it was now giving up. In addition it gained some advantage from the fact that Austria and Switzerland as neighbouring states would now create a larger gap in the north–south line of NATO, from Norway to Italy. But the essential change was that one of the major relics of the war had been eliminated.

The atmosphere of Europe seemed to be changing, and in the summer of 1955 there occurred the first summit meeting to take place since the Potsdam Conference of 1945. The heads of the four great powers which had conquered Germany met in Geneva in an attempt to negotiate a more far-reaching settlement of the German question and of European security. Few people held any great hopes that specific agreements would be reached—although the example of Austria suggested that it was not impossible. But it was widely believed that something would be gained if the leaders of the great powers met each other. It was hoped that they would find some common ground, and that an accord, however small, might escalate into peace.

The concrete achievements of the Geneva summit were indeed small. It rapidly became apparent that the settlement of the Far-eastern wars and the liquidation of small-scale problems like that of Austria did not make it any easier to arrive at a solution of the major problem of Germany in the centre of Europe. The Western powers stood firm on their insistence that there should be free elections as a means to the reunification of Germany. The Russians, in contrast, showed signs of a new policy which became more definite after the conference—instead of talking of German reunification, as they had done in an attempt to discourage the union of West Germany to western Europe, they now sought to create two Germanies, and to secure acceptance of a German Federal Republic and a German Democratic Republic as two separate independent states.

It was the atmosphere rather than the agreements of Geneva which appeared most significant; but the "Geneva spirit" soon evaporated. When the heads of state departed and foreign ministers were left to carry on detailed negotiations the depth of disagreement was more obvious than the extent of agreement. In the autumn it became known that the Czech government had negotiated the sale of a large quantity of arms to Egypt—the beginning of major Soviet involvement in Middle-Eastern affairs and a clear sign to some that the leopard had not changed his spots. It was above all in eastern Europe that the thaw of 1955 was most effectively refrozen in the following year: but in the long run it proved that the biggest developments were taking place in that very area.

An important part of the new Soviet policy was the decision of Khrushchev and Bulganin to bring about a reconciliation with Tito. In May 1955 they travelled to Belgrade for this purpose—a significant event in itself, that the leaders of one of the superpowers should go to the capital of a minor power. Going even further, Khrushchev made a speech recognizing Soviet errors in the origin of the dispute with Yugoslavia. At the end of the visit, at the beginning of June, an agreement was signed on the Yugoslav terms —it was a formal agreement between the heads of state, not a fraternal one between two Communist parties. The following year the Cominform was dissolved, because it was the instrument through which Stalin had worked in eastern Europe, and had formally expelled Yugoslavia. When this had been done Tito returned the Russian leaders' visit and went to the Soviet Union. He received a hero's reception, and began to see himself as playing a major role in the formulation of policy for the whole Soviet bloc.

Meanwhile, Khrushchev had taken the revaluation of Stalinism much further. In February 1956 he addressed the Twentieth Congress of the Communist Party of the Soviet Union. One speech he made was secret; but the text of it was obtained by American intelligence and published—although it could not circulate in the Soviet Union. It was this speech which consisted entirely of a denunciation of Stalin and Stalinist rule. Khrushchev accused Stalin of perverting communism by the "cult of personality"—by his own personal, dictatorial rule. He denounced the purges and terror of Stalinist rule, and denied Stalin's claims to be a great war leader.

The significance of the speech can only be judged when it is remembered that the Communist system had built up a strong pyramid of authority, with Stalin at its pinnacle. Communist ideology claimed to be a truly scientific account of world history and development; the Communist party of the Soviet Union claimed to interpret Communist ideology, and Stalin to be the all-wise leader of the party. Once Stalin's authority was undermined by his former lieutenant and now his successor, the whole system of Communist authority was threatened.

The secret speech was not the only one which Khrushchev made at the Congress. In addition to denouncing Stalinist rule he made two further significant revaluations of Communist doctrine. He rejected the old idea that war between the Socialist and the Imperialist sections of the world was inevitable. He argued that the isolation of the Soviet Union no longer endangered its existence, that it was surrounded by "peace-loving" states—the newly independent states of Africa and Asia—and that communism could spread without inevitable war. Khrushchev and other leaders also now admitted what followed logically from the reconciliation with Yugoslavia—that there was not a single path to socialism, and that different Communist parties might achieve power in different ways.

It was Khrushchev's intention to achieve a reconstruction of government in the Soviet Union and the relations between the countries in the Soviet bloc in controlled stages—hence the importance of secrecy in a speech intended only for the ruling élite of the party. Within the Soviet Union much had been done to dismantle the apparatus of the police state. The police chief, Beria, had, it is thought, been prevented from trying to take power himself and had been executed. In the Soviet bloc a new institution had been created by the signature of the Warsaw Pact in 1955. The pact was intended as a riposte to the agreement on Western European Union and was phrased in internationally respectable terms, with much reference to the United Nations. It did not make any important immediate changes in the military position of Russia in eastern Europe, but it did make formal provision for a Joint Command and a Political Consultative Committee. Together with a revitalized Comecon it was intended to provide a new framework which would retain firm control from the top but permit a greater degree of consultation.

But in 1956 events took charge of themselves. The reconciliation with Tito meant that in other countries of the Soviet bloc those leaders who had been disgraced at the time of the Soviet–Yugoslav split were now rehabilitated—provided that they had not been executed. In Hungary, Imre Nagy had re-emerged and taken over the government immediately after Stalin's death, until April 1955; in Poland, Gomulka was released from prison and began rapidly to regain his ascendancy in the Polish Communist party. These were men who could not but be impressed by Tito's record and would seek to emulate him, in so far as was possible given the weaker position of a country such as Poland in its geographical relation to the Soviet Union.

More important was the fact that the ferment of ideas, the changes in leadership and in the government of the Soviet Union, together with the introduction of new economic policies, produced growing unrest in important groups of ordinary citizens. The people most affected were those who had been the traditional supporters of revolution in nineteenth-century Europe—students and intellectuals who looked for greater freedom, and workers whose wages and standards of living were directly affected by economic policies. In Poland and in Hungary in the summer and autumn of 1956 these movements of protest and the attempt to shake off constraints grew into open riot and revolt.

The course of events differed in the two countries. In Poland riots occurred in the town of Poznan in June, at a time when Gomulka was re-establishing his ascendancy in the Communist party. By the end of the summer the Gomulka group were in firm control, and commanded the country through the security forces and the army. The Poznan rioters were brought to trial, but few were convicted and sentences were minor. Popular uprising had facilitated a change of leadership over which the Russians were unable to exercise any control. Briefly they tried to intervene. Khrushchev and his principal lieutenants flew to Warsaw and demanded that their men in the Polish party be reinstated. But the Poles stood firm and resisted the Russian demands, and they were in a position to do so unless the Russians were prepared to resort to force on a large scale. Khrushchev and his team flew back to Moscow having achieved nothing; the Polish-born but Russian Marshal of the Polish forces, Rokossovski, was dismissed. A national Communist government had successfully claimed a measure of independence from the Soviet Union.

By this time events in Hungary were moving to a climax. The upsurge of revolution brought Imre Nagy back to power, but then continued unabated and passed out of the control of the government. It seems probable that the Soviet government may have come to terms with Nagy as they had with Gomulka—had Nagy been able to command the country. Their troops had intervened once in Budapest, and then withdrawn, while fresh forces gathered in the east of the country. Meanwhile the old non-Communist political parties had reappeared, and at the end of October a coalition government was formed, including the names of non-Communists who had been excluded from power since 1947. On 1 November a telegram was sent to the Secretary-General of the United Nations requesting support for Hungary's neutrality.

Meanwhile a former colleague of Nagy, Janos Kadar, had joined forces with the Russians, and shown himself willing to head a new Hungarian government installed by the Russians. Soviet troops now moved once again into Budapest, and against resolute and determined opposition suppressed the Hungarian revolt. Nagy sought

UNE—D

refuge in the Yugoslav embassy (and was later executed) and a new government under Kadar established in his place.

The tragic heroism of the Hungarian people made a deep impact outside the Soviet bloc, especially as a fresh wave of refugees fled from Hungary westwards. They were respected and admired for their desperate bid for freedom, and the Soviet government bitterly condemned in western Europe. It might have been possible for Western governments to take advantage of the revolts in Poland and Hungary to bring a loosening of Soviet control in eastern Europe, had they been prepared to use a skilful combination of threats, diplomacy, and offers to negotiate a large neutralist settlement—for they were certainly not prepared to initiate a new war in Europe for the sake of Hungary. But their preoccupations were elsewhere. As a result of Nasser's nationalization of the Suez canal, British and French troops were engaged in a joint attack, in alliance with Israel, on Egypt. They were in no position to take action in Europe, and the Western alliance was split wide open by the opposition of the United States to the British and French action. In any case Dulles would have been unlikely to favour neutralism in Europe.

It appeared, therefore, that the outcome of the revolt was the installation of a new puppet manipulated by the Russians in Hungary, and this appearance was confirmed in the following year when Soviet policy in eastern Europe was again tightened and a fresh dispute with Yugoslavia began. But appearances were deceptive. Although Hungary remained a Communist country it came increasingly to show, that, like Poland, it would pursue an independent policy at least in its domestic economic policies.

Moreover, a change of fundamental significance had come about in European politics. As a result of Khrushchev's policies and the tide of events, national Communist governments had emerged in eastern Europe. The myth of Communist unity was broken—it was soon to be totally destroyed by increasingly violent hostility between Russia and China. The Stalinist system of coercion and control had been broken down and Communist governments could take their own decisions without reference to Moscow—even though common interest bound most of them to their powerful neighbour.

The change was of wider significance. The Communist parties of western Europe also gained a new independence. They ceased to be the agents of Moscow and could devise the best methods for themselves in the pursuit of power in their own countries. The more that this happened, the more readily were they accepted into their national political framework. At the same time in western Europe hostility to the Communist bloc diminished, once it was accepted that Russia had no longer an obedient force owing allegiance primarily to Moscow rather than to its own national government. Thus, although the immediate result of the Hungarian Revolution and its suppression was to freeze Europe and renew the atmosphere of the Cold War, the long-term effect of the changes of 1953–6 was to weaken the barrier to unity in Europe as a whole.

# CHAPTER 6

# EEC, de Gaulle, and Britain

WHEN the European Defence Community collapsed in the summer of 1954 many predicted that the movement to the close union of western Europe was dead—that the strain imposed on it by an attempt to integrate defence forces was more than it could bear. Those who believed in union, however, regarded it as a challenge. Jean Monnet, who more than any one else had been the motive force behind European integration, resigned from the presidency of the High Authority of the Coal and Steel Community in order to campaign actively for a united Europe.

At the beginning of June 1955 governmental action was also resumed. A meeting of the foreign ministers of the Six met at Messina in Italy to devise means for further integration of the western European economy. The opportunity was open for the British government to participate in these discussions and to enter the European community now that it was beginning on a fresh phase in its integration. It chose not to do so. It sent a representative to Messina—something more than an observer, but less than a delegate. As discussions proceeded it was evident that there were fundamental differences between Britain and the Six, and British representation ceased by the end of 1955.

Left to themselves—for no other western European government tried to join them—the Six worked throughout 1956 to produce two treaties, which were signed at Rome in March 1957. The first of the treaties established a European Economic Community (EEC) —more easily known as the Common Market, and the second a European Atomic Energy Community, concerned with the integrated development of atomic energy for peaceful uses. The Common Market, as provided for under the treaty, was to be far more than a free-trade area; it was to become a community closely integrated in all its most central economic and social policies—an objective which has been largely achieved within the timetable laid down.

The treaty itself is one of the longest to be negotiated, consisting of some 248 articles. It starts with an outline of principles—a summary of what is included more specifically in the following articles —and a timetable by which the objectives of the treaty should be achieved over the next twelve years. The first massive part of this programme, elaborated in the next set of articles, provides for the free movement of goods—the elimination of duties and quantitive restrictions between members of the Community, and the establishment of a common tariff on goods coming from outside the Community. Special provision is then made for agriculture, with the supposition that agriculture should not be completely free from governmental arrangements, but that these arrangements should be the same throughout the Common Market—in short there should be a common agricultural policy. The treaty next provides for the free movement of persons, services, and capital within the Common Market and for a common transport policy. It recognizes that once restrictions are removed the member countries will be subject to unfair competition amongst themselves if their social policies— pensions and social insurance, unemployment benefits—are out of line with each other. It therefore provides for "harmonization" in this area, and establishes a European Social Fund to assist with the retraining and reallocation of labour. It also provides for the association of overseas countries and territories with the Common Market. Finally the treaty provides for the establishment of institutions for the government of the Community.

These institutions are similar in broad shape to those of the Coal and Steel Community. An important difference, however, is to be found in that the equivalent of the High Authority of the Coal and Steel Community is called the Commission, and is not given the same supranational position as is the High Authority. It is given the task of ensuring that the provisions of the treaty are carried out, and it also has the power of putting up proposals to the Council of Ministers. This latter power of initiation has been of great importance, since the Council can only amend the Commission's proposals if it is unanimous. The Council of Ministers is similar to that for the Coal and Steel Community, with the important provision that after seven years voting in the Council should be by majority— a clause which the French government of de Gaulle later refused to comply with. The treaty also set up a Court of Justice, which became common to the Coal and Steel Community and the Atomic Energy Community; and an assembly, which also became common to all three and was called the European Parliament.

At this stage the British government was not prepared to enter on commitments of such a far-reaching nature. During the negotiations for the setting up of the EEC it had pursued an alternative policy aimed at the creation of a free-trade area.

Support for British policy was sufficient within OEEC for a committee to be set up under the chairmanship of Reginald Maudling to explore the possibility of a free-trade area in Europe. But its discussions not only produced no positive results for western Europe as a whole but aroused considerable suspicion of British motives in Europe. The avowed policy of the British government was the establishment of a free-trade area in which the Common Market would have a place; inevitably its action gave the impression of an attempt to defeat the Common Market negotiations.

Instead of the OEEC becoming a new free-trade association, it developed into a new organization with the deceptively similar initials, OECD. This organization, which came into being in 1960, was for Economic Co-operation and Development. It ceased to be a purely European grouping and embraced the United States and Japan. Its principal function came to be the provision of statistical and other information valuable to the advanced industrial countries belonging to it and the co-ordination of aid given to the developing countries.

When it was clear that a free-trade area for the whole of western Europe would not be achieved the British government did not abandon the idea altogether. Instead they joined with six other like-minded governments, and brought a new grouping into existence—the European Free Trade Association (EFTA). The members of the Association are the Scandinavian countries (Sweden, Norway, and Denmark), Portugal, Austria, and Switzerland, as well as Britain—seven countries which between them have a smaller proportion of western Europe's inhabitants and industries than do the Six of the Common Market. EFTA was established by the signature of a convention in Stockholm and came into being in May 1960. Its members undertook to remove quantitive restrictions and tariffs on trade in industrial goods progressively over the next six years. The agreement did not cover agricultural goods, except that it encouraged agreements between members and forbade agricultural policies harmful to other members of the Association. It did not seek to establish a common external tariff. It did not set up a complicated institutional arrangement, but it did establish a Council, in which each member has one representative and one vote, decisions being taken unanimously.

EFTA has had great importance in the development of the European economy, in promoting industrial free trade between its members, furthering agricultural co-operation, and increasing trade in the prepared agricultural products like tinned sardines. On the other hand it was never intended, as the Common Market was, to be a stepping stone towards close political integration. The progress which EFTA made was matched by that of the Common Market. The stresses and strains which were so prominent in western Europe in 1957 disappeared, especially after the devaluation of the French franc in 1958, so that the Common Market was able to carry out its programme of tariff reductions and the establishment of a common external tariff in advance of the agreed timetable. In these circumstances the success of EFTA, important as it was, did not turn it into an organization which could bargain with EEC from a position of strength.

During the period when substantial progress was thus being made in European integration the European powers were engaged in a series of manœuvres which they were only partially able to control, as a result of which they gave up almost the entirety of their former overseas empires. The first round in this process of decolonization had begun shortly after the Second World War. Britain had given independence to India, Pakistan, Ceylon, and Burma; Holland had abandoned Indonesia, and the French had embarked on the long war in Indo-China which finally resulted in their withdrawal in 1954. For the French the second round followed immediately after the first, for as the war in Indo-China ended revolt in Algeria began. In 1957 Britain gave independence to Ghana, then to Malaya, and embarked on the policy which would bring independence and African majorities to the states of central and eastern Africa—except Rhodesia. The failure of the Suez expedition and the 1958 revolution in Iraq rapidly accelerated the curtailment of the British position in the Middle East. Meanwhile, France gave independence to Morocco and Tunisia by 1956 and made preparations for the independence of its colonies south of the Sahara. The Congo became independent of Belgium in 1960—only to be involved in drawn-out internal disorder into which the United Nations was drawn.

Decolonization had a dual effect on European developments. On the one hand it concentrated the attention of the European states on European affairs as they curtailed their world interests. This process happened sharply with France after the end of the Algerian War, partly because French interests in Europe had always taken priority. With Britain, traditionally a world power separated from the continent, it happened more slowly. At the same time the war in Algeria had the coincidental effect of bringing General de Gaulle to power in France, and thus establishing for the first time since the war a strong government with an alternative vision of the future of Europe to that of the Federalists—and one resolutely opposed to the close alliance of Europe to the United States.

Revolution began in Algeria in 1954 and soon grew into a major war which the governments of the Fourth Republic were unable to bring to an end. It was impossible to achieve military victory with the forces available—indeed it may have been impossible whatever forces could be deployed because of the nature of guerrilla warfare. But equally the governments of the Fourth Republic lacked the political authority to achieve a settlement with the Algerian nationalists. The French army in Algeria had acquired a sense of independence very rare in democratic societies. Its officers included men who had experienced the conflict of loyalty between occupied Vichy France and the resistance; subsequently they had gone through the humiliating failure to achieve victory in Indo-China before being transferred to Algeria. Many of them had lived for years outside France, isolated from its normal political life, and had come to think of the army as a body better fitted to decide the affairs of the nation than the parliament or the government of the discredited Fourth Republic. They believed that military victory was possible in Algeria, and in spite of the methods of torture used by some army units in the conduct of the war, many of them had a sense of a civilizing mission of an old-fashioned imperial kind.

Relations between the army and the French settlers in Algeria were not normally very close—the army had no greater respect for French civilians in Algeria than in France itself. But in extreme circumstances the common interest of these two groups in the achievement of victory brought them together. This happened in May 1958 when a sudden *coup* by the army took over the machinery of government in Algeria. But neither the army nor the settlers had plans or could provide a leader to extend their revolution from Algeria to France itself. Instead they looked for leadership to the one man who had consistently spoken of the need for strong government in France and who was himself an officer—General de Gaulle.

The government of the Fourth Republic lacked the means to counter the Algerian *coup*, and their dominant aim was to avert civil war and maintain the institutions of the Republic intact. They too, therefore, were prepared to accept de Gaulle's leadership. For them de Gaulle was the man who had led the liberation of France and restored the Republic in 1945. De Gaulle himself meanwhile judged that the occasion had arrived for which he had waited since 1946—the moment when he could return to power and effect the salvation of his country. He therefore played his cards with the utmost political skill in order to be able to take power as he wanted it, maintaining on the one hand the support of the army and avoiding on the other any offence to the susceptibilities of the politicians.

Anxious days were passed as it appeared that French paratroopers were ready to land from Algeria in France and as de Gaulle conducted negotiations with the President and Ministers of the Fourth Republic. Then on 29 May 1958 it was announced that President Coty had asked de Gaulle to form a government. As a result de Gaulle came back to power in a constitutional manner as Prime Minister of the Fourth Republic. A new constitution was devised and de Gaulle was then elected President of the Fifth French Republic. In this way he acquired great political authority. The constitution of the Fifth Republic gave him far stronger powers than any Prime Minister or President had enjoyed in France since 1870. Because he came to power legally and constitutionally he could take a strong stand on legality when he was faced with any new insurrection—as happened in 1961 when the army in Algeria attempted a further unsuccessful *coup*. He enjoyed too a great reserve of authority since the French people viewed with alarm the possibility of de Gaulle's departure and a second return to at best the weakness of the Fourth Republic and at worst possible civil war and dictatorship.

De Gaulle used this position of strength to move steadily towards a settlement of the Algerian War based on the self-determination of the people of Algeria. The million Frenchmen living there were outnumbered by eight times as many Muslims, so that this could only lead to Algerian independence. It is understandable that it took four years, from the time de Gaulle came to power in 1958 until 1962, to bring this about. But when Algeria became independent France was free for the first time since 1946 from colonial wars which had been costly and had limited the manœuvrability of its foreign policy.

During his first five years of power de Gaulle's influences on the development of European and Atlantic institutions were significant pointers to the future rather than of fundamental importance in themselves. Both France and Europe lived in a prolonged atmosphere of crisis. The Algerian War lasted as long after de Gaulle's accession to power as it had before. In Europe crisis was provoked by the initiative of Khrushchev's government in insisting that a resettlement must be made of Germany. Starting in November 1958 he brought continuous pressure to bear on the United States, Britain, and France to alter the status of Berlin—one proposal was that it should be a "free city"—and conclude a peace treaty with the German Democratic Republic. The threat with which he backed up his pressure was that Russia would make a separate treaty with East Germany, and hand over control of the access to Berlin. This would then undermine the Western position in the city, which the Western powers insisted followed on four-power agreements at the end of the war—agreements which had never been superseded by a peace treaty.

The Western powers were intent on maintaining their position in Berlin. They did so in order to protect the rights and interests of the West Berliners, rather than allow them against their will to be placed under Communist rule. The Russians offered no concessions in return for the demands which they made—and the Western powers viewed with grave suspicion proposals for a free city with a United Nations presence. In addition Berlin was a useful advance post in the Communist empire. It provided a means by which East Germans could escape to the west—and this was no doubt a major reason why Khrushchev and the government of the German Democratic Republic wanted to effect a change.

The crisis had a certain artificiality in that it was provoked by the Russians and ended when they chose not to press further. But it was no less intense for being artificial. It reached its climax in August 1961 when the East Germans constructed a concrete wall separating East from West Berlin, thereby preventing any travel by Germans from east to west—although the four occupying powers continued to go back and forth as their duties required. Both sides in the dispute strengthened their forces in Germany and the leadership of those forces in a way that might well have led to war in an earlier century. At one time the opposing tanks faced each other point-blank across the dividing line in Berlin. Except for the building of the wall, which had a permanent effect in severing communication between east and west, neither side forced the issue. The Western powers did not try to knock the wall down, as some said they should; the Russians abandoned their stated intention of signing a separate peace treaty.

From the start there had been a strong sense of ebb and flow in the crisis. The Russians' initial note in November 1958 had demanded a fresh settlement of Berlin and Germany within six months, but as that period approached its close they made clear that they had not issued an "ultimatum". In 1959 Krushchev visited the United States and had cordial talks with President Eisenhower; in 1960 a summit meeting was arranged to take place in Paris, but Krushchev abruptly broke it up because an American reconnaissance aeroplane (a U-2) had been shot down over the Soviet Union, and the United States government admitted that it had been engaged in intelligence photography. The next year the crisis in Berlin itself reached its peak, and in 1962 the anniversary of the building of the wall passed off without any settlement—but without renewed danger.

Instead the flashpoint of the world moved across the Atlantic to Cuba. The government of Fidel Castro, who had fought his way to power in January 1959, was regarded by the United States as a growing danger to Latin America. The Americans supported a disastrous attempt on the part of the Cuban refugees to invade the island and eject Castro. Then in 1962 their intelligence services and aerial photography showed that the Russians were installing missiles in Cuba capable of penetrating to the heart of the United States.

The government of President Kennedy insisted that the missiles be removed. In an atmosphere of the most acute tension they instituted a naval blockade of the island, and mobilized overwhelming supporting force lest their demands should not be met. Krushchev and Kennedy exchanged notes in which each recognized the responsibility which they held as the heads of superpowers with nuclear capability, and a "hot line" was established for direct communication between Moscow and Washington.

While the Berlin and Cuban crises lasted, and while France was preoccupied with the Algerian War, economic integration proceeded unobtrusively but uninterrupted. NATO was actively concerned with the Berlin crisis, and the United States government sent

Dean Acheson to explain to its European allies the moves it was making over Cuba. Clearly it was the readiness of the United States to defend Berlin—as shown by the movement of its troops—which was decisive, and NATO was told rather than asked about Cuba, over which American interests predominated.

Meanwhile an indication of future developments could be found both in the views de Gaulle expressed and was known to hold, and in the initiatives he took with regard to NATO. De Gaulle was and remains an exponent of French nationalism. He regards the nation state as the form of political organization which most closely corresponds to political reality. It alone commands the loyalty of peoples, and is the only organization which controls political power. Lesser institutions are subordinate to the state, and the state cannot delegate its authority or its sovereignty to any international organization. Nation states enhance the dignity and importance of their citizens—and with no country is this more so than with France. As de Gaulle wrote at the beginning of his war memoirs: "France is not really herself unless she is in the front rank. . . . France cannot be France without greatness."

In the Gaullist view nation states have certain permanent and enduring interests. Temporarily these may be obscured by the rush of events or they may be overlaid by ideology; but they will reassert themselves. Similarly, ideology may for a time command the allegiance of peoples—but in a transitory way, until nationalism reasserts itself.

Important consequences follow from these presuppositions. The organization of NATO is doubly condemned. It is condemned because it subordinates national defence to an international organization which cannot have the strength of a nation state; and it is condemned because it gives power in European affairs to two countries whose interests are in the world rather than Europe—Britain and the United States. The alliance has a basic reality, since in the last resort western Europe and the United States may be fighting on the same side. But except in an ultimate crisis France has common interests with the states of eastern Europe—European states like itself, whose strong national interests provide the possibility of co-operation with

France once the temporary barrier of ideological difference has disappeared. Europe should be strengthened, for its own sake and as a counter to the United States—but to suppose that it can be strengthened by the development of supranational institutions is again to be drawn off into unreality.

This radical view of the course French policy should take revealed itself soon after de Gaulle came to power. In 1958 he addressed a note to Britain and the United States suggesting a revision of the structure of NATO, giving it a super-directorate of the three powers, America, Britain, and France. The next year French naval forces in the Mediterranean were withdrawn from NATO command, in war as well as peace, and the United States was no longer allowed by France to stockpile nuclear weapons on French soil. The French government pressed ahead with the development of its own nuclear weapons, which had been begun under the Fourth Republic, with the intention of giving them a greater importance as an indication of independent policy than earlier governments had envisaged. This was the beginning of a policy which was to be more amply developed in later years.

Meanwhile the British experience of decolonization was proceeding more peacefully than that of France. The Conservative government which was returned to power under the premiership of Harold Macmillan in 1959 recognized the impossibility of maintaining imperial rule against the demands of African nationalism. But to transfer power to Africans in east and central Africa was a complex task. The pattern was similar to that of Algeria in that a European minority, largely of British descent, had settled and established their homes. This European minority was in a dominant position over the Africans in that it possessed the greater part of the wealth of the country and occupied the top position in government and business administration. It would have been relatively simple for the British government to hand over power to this minority—but to do so would only have postponed the problem of African nationalism and the demands of the Africans for majority rule. The emotional ties which the British felt towards Africa were weaker than those which bound the French to Algeria. The British government had no intention of preserving the privileges of the European minority.

The situation was complicated further by the fact that in 1953 the British government had constituted a Federation in Central Africa of the three territories of Southern and Northern Rhodesia and Nyasaland. The arguments in favour of such a Federation were largely economic and were based on the belief that the prosperity of the area would be enhanced by an economic union. But it also had obvious political implications. It was favoured by the European minority who dominated the government of the Federation and who were in the best position to take advantage of it; it had always been resisted by the Africans for the same reason. Some years later when the Africans had taken over power in Northern Rhodesia and Nyasaland it became apparent that they might have been wiser to support the Federation as a means of gaining control of Southern Rhodesia. But at the time African opinion was strongly opposed to federation.

Another difficulty arose in the fact that another of the east African territories, Kenya, had experienced an outbreak of particularly savage violence in the Mau-Mau movement which lasted for some five years from October 1952. The Mau-Mau movement was a combination of African hostility to European rule, and primitive, emotional violence which flourished in an atmosphere of secrecy and oath-taking. It might have been expected therefore that the resistance to African demands would be that much greater since governments in power are normally reluctant to share power with those who use violence until they are forced to do so.

In spite of these difficulties the policy of the British government was made clear by Macmillan as Prime Minister in a speech he made on 3 February 1960:

> Ever since the breakup of the Roman Empire one of the constant facts of political life in Europe has been the emergence of independent nations. . . . Fifteen years ago this movement spread through Asia. Many countries there, of different races and civilization, pressed their claim to an independent national life. To-day the same thing is happening in Africa. The most striking of all the impressions I have formed

since I left London a month ago is of the strength of this national consciousness. In different places it may take different forms, but it is happening everywhere. The wind of change is blowing through the continent.[1]

Significantly the speech was made to the parliament of South Africa—a country in which the Afrikaans and British minority enjoyed precisely that monopoly of power which it was the government's intention to avoid in east Africa.

In spite of complications and difficulties—and to the surprise of the British government—it proved possible to devise new constitutions for the countries of east Africa, except Southern Rhodesia, and prepare the way for independence on the basis of these constitutions. The government accepted the breakup of the Central African Federation so that Northern Rhodesia became the independent state of Zambia and Nyasaland became Malawi; Kenya and Tanganyika were already independent—the latter joining Zanzibar to become Tanzania.

All these new states became members of the Commonwealth but they did so at the cost of one of the older members—South Africa. There the maintenance of white supremacy was associated with a virulent form of Afrikaans nationalism which would in any case have led the South African government to make a demonstration of independence from Britain. This demonstration took the form of a South African Republic, with the consequence that South Africa had to apply for readmission to the Commonwealth under its new form of government. But the pressure brought on the government both at the United Nations and at Commonwealth meetings to change its policy of apartheid was such that it decided not to seek such readmission. Its decision was taken in the course of the Commonwealth Prime Ministers' Conference of 1961.

To many people, particularly in the Labour party, the Commonwealth appeared a more important and more successful institution now that it included African members. But the Conservative government was aware of the difficulties of holding together what promised to become a very large grouping of states with inde-

[1] P. N. S. Mansergh, *Documents and Speeches on Commonwealth Affairs, 1952–62*, p. 347.

pendent and conflicting interests, particularly in foreign policy. The attitude of the two parties towards the Commonwealth had reversed itself—it was now the Labour party which was the strongest supporter of the maintenance of the Commonwealth as an institution.

For the Macmillan government the growing dispersion of the Commonwealth made a European policy more important—at a time when two other forces were pulling strongly in the same direction. The first was the success of the Common Market in developing its institutions while at the same time enjoying a period of great economic growth. This contrasted sharply with the persistent difficulties which the British government encountered in solving its balance of payments difficulties and pursuing a steady economic policy instead of "stop–go". For so long the British had held aloof from European integration because they did not expect it to succeed; now they found themselves in the position of weakness. As Jean Monnet was reported to have said: "It is impossible to interest the English in an idea, but fortunately they will always face facts."

The second factor of importance in British policy was the apparent weakening of the special relationship with the United States. In the days after the war it had been a cardinal point of Bevin's foreign policy that Britain should form a link between the United States and Europe. The close wartime co-operation between the two countries had established ties that did not quickly disappear, in spite of differences of policy. NATO embodied an Anglo-American relationship which was particularly strong while France was involved in war in Indo-China. But the success of the Common Market impressed the United States. The new American administration under President Kennedy, which came into office in January 1961, did not take for granted that there should be an Anglo-American special relationship, and saw the necessity for American interests of close relations with Europe. The American government therefore let the British know that if Europe were at sixes and sevens —divided between the Common Market countries and those of EFTA—the United States would be on the side of the Six. But what it would most strongly favour was an integrated Europe including Britain. The Western alliance would then take the shape of a dumbbell across the Atlantic—a strong Europe balancing a strong United States. It was this concept which Kennedy had in mind when he later used the occasion of Independence Day (4 July 1962) to make a "declaration of interdependence".

The three most basic factors which had kept Britain aloof from Europe had thus changed. The Common Market was a success, Commonwealth ties were loosening, and the special relationship had come to depend to some extent on Britain joining Europe. It was in these circumstances that, as Prime Minister, Macmillan announced to the House of Commons on 31 July 1961 that Britain would seek entry to the Common Market.

An application on the part of Britain to join the Common Market inevitably required long negotiations. It had taken more than a year to negotiate the Rome Treaty, and the difficulties were no less when Britain sought to join its economy to the Common Market, itself in the course of development. Britain's trade was predominantly directed towards the world rather than Europe; its system of agricultural protection was different from that of the Common Market countries—it relied on price support rather than tariffs—and it had special arrangements with the Commonwealth countries. The Common Market countries sought to protect their own national interests as well as those of the Community itself; Britain wished to safeguard its own position and to soften the blow which its entry must cause the Commonwealth—especially New Zealand, with the closest emotional ties to Britain and the most important of its markets there.

In spite of the obstacles to be overcome negotiations made progress. They were broken off for the summer in 1962, and resumed thereafter. By this time the Algerian War had come to an end, and de Gaulle was able to concentrate his attention on Europe. In doing so he succeeded in establishing closer ties between France and Germany. He visited the erstwhile enemy of France, and received a stirring welcome from the German crowds. He had already formed a close attachment to Adenauer, which was enhanced still further by his visit. He was beginning to shape Europe in accordance with his own beliefs. Instead of integration he was working towards a confederal Europe, its unity forged by periodic meetings of heads of state, revolving round Franco-German co-operation—with France playing the leading role.

Britain would not fit easily into such a scheme. Anglo-French rivalry has been the most persistent theme in European history for a longer period than any other quarrel has been sustained; and in de Gaulle's mind Britain was not a European country. Ever since 1941, in de Gaulle's view, the British had worked in partnership with the United States in pursuit of their own interests and the diminution of France. They had engineered the break-up of the French Empire, whether for the extension of their own power and influence or on more ideological grounds, and they had sought to impose their will on Europe, at Yalta and Potsdam, without consulting the French. In spite of Britain's application to join the Common Market and the concessions which it had made in detailed negotiations, de Gaulle may have remained unconvinced.

Then at the end of 1962 occurred a series of events which brought the possibility of British entry to an end. They sprang from extraneous circumstances, and are an example of how grand strategies in politics may be defeated by small causes. For budgetary reasons the United States decided not to go ahead with the production of an air to ground missile, the Skybolt. In the United States armoury this was of relatively little importance, because the more effective Polaris missile had been successfully developed. But the decision affected Britain quite disproportionately. The British government had abandoned the development of a missile of its own as being too expensive, and had negotiated the supply of Skybolt from the United States instead. The decision not to go ahead with Skybolt therefore threatened the whole British policy of an independent nuclear deterrent. At any other time it might have been possible to surmount the consequent difficulties unobtrusively. But the political position of the Macmillan government was relatively weak. It had carried through the programme of decolonization in Africa against the opposition of the right wing of the party, and it was engaged in negotiating British entry into the Common Market, involving important sacrifices and the abandonment of cherished sovereignty. In addition it was now put in the position of being forced to surrender the independent deterrent. To make the problem more complex the United States was opposed to the proliferation of nuclear weapons, and was unlikely to negotiate a fresh arrangement with the British without some safeguards of its position.

The Prime Minister flew to Nassau in the Bahamas for a meeting with the President of the United States, and an agreement was worked out between the two governments for the supply of Polaris missiles to Britain—with the provision that the submarine carrying them should form part of a NATO force except when "supreme national interests are at stake".

The problem of Britain's independent deterrent had thus been resolved—but at the cost of entry to the Common Market. It was open to France to make a similar agreement with the United States, but de Gaulle had no intention of doing so. The Nassau experience confirmed him in his view of the relationship between Britain and America. Instead of sharing in nuclear development with France, a European power, the British Prime Minister had gone immediately to the United States when British interests were at stake, had signed an agreement which confirmed British dependence on the United States, and included a formula for NATO nuclear deterrence which de Gaulle, given his views of NATO, considered quite unrealistic.

Abruptly the negotiations which had been going on at Brussels were broken off in January 1963. Britain's first application to join Europe had failed. Shortly afterwards France and Germany signed a treaty of co-operation.

# CHAPTER 7

# After the Veto—Britain
# Tries Again

DE GAULLE's veto on the British entry into the Common Market had an impact on the internal politics of the Common Market almost as great as its effect on relations with Britain. Formally France was fully within its powers in the action it had taken but there was no doubt in the minds of the other members of the Community that the spirit of the Community had been dealt a severe blow by such unilateral action. Moreover the Franco-German treaty suggested a relationship between two members of the Community whose future was difficult to evaluate. On the one hand Franco-German co-operation was indispensable to the successful development of the Community; on the other hand Franco-German hegemony in Europe could only destroy the balance of the Community as a whole.

The question at issue in the future development of Europe had always been whether the momentum of the three Communities, especially EEC, would surmount the old form of nationalism and create political union. This question took a more acute form now that nationalism was galvanized under Gaullist leadership.

The momentum of the Community derived from three main sources. In the first place the implementation of the Rome Treaty established its own momentum. The Community actually went faster than the treaty had envisaged in the reduction of internal tariffs and making uniform the external tariff. The inevitable result of this was that industrialists in the Community made their plans on the assumption that the Community would continue to develop. Governments, too, especially the French government with its complex and efficient system of national planning, worked from the assumption that there would be a Common Market and, once having done so, had an obvious interest in bringing the Common Market into existence.

These tendencies were strengthened when the Community had to negotiate with other countries. The timetable for establishing a common front towards the outside world was speeded up whenever the initiative of other countries forced quick decisions on the Community. This was true of Britain's application to join the Common Market. Although in the end the application came to nothing, while it was under consideration it accelerated agreement between the six countries to make possible an agreement between themselves and the would-be newcomer to the Community. The need in 1964 to negotiate with other members of the General Agreement on Tariffs and Trade for worldwide reduction of tariffs had a similar effect in accelerating the movement towards uniformity amongst the Common Market countries. The pattern of tariffs amongst the European countries was different from that of Britain and America—in the former case all tariffs were grouped together in a range from about 10 per cent to 20 per cent, whereas in the latter there were greater extremes of very low and very high tariffs. These differences made for hard bargaining between the two and the Common Market countries were in a better position to bargain if they could harmonize their own tariffs first.

Of all the features promoting the development of the Community the institutions of the Community were, however, the most powerful of all. By 1963 these had achieved a stable existence and a firm purpose of their own which rapidly recovered from the setback of the de Gaulle veto. The core of the Community's institutions was to be found in the Commission, which, in addition to its own authority, could wield great influence and power by putting forward proposals to the Council of Ministers. The Commission quickly showed that it was made up of a skilful body of men. It was backed by a powerful civil service of its own—in March 1966 there were some 3300 employees of the Community in Brussels. It took care to practise "the art of the possible" and to make proposals which would move the Community forward to the extent it thought possible in view of the natural hesitation of national governments (although it signally failed to do this in 1965).

To facilitate its work the Community set up management committees, each concerned with a particular group of commodities about which decisions had to be taken, on which national interests were represented. Moreover, it was possible for the Commission to present its proposals to the Assembly of the Community and to the press at the same time as it sent them to the Council of Ministers. In this way it could both take account of national interests in framing its proposals and make the most of the opportunity to build up favourable opinion in its support. Whether this balance of interests and the power of initiative vested in the Commission could be given the grand name of "supranational" had ceased to be important. No one could deny or ignore the fact that European politics, with all the accompaniment of public relations and group pressures, had come into existence, and the members of the Commission and the Assembly were strongly committed to the further development of the Community.

There was therefore considerable momentum towards greater union. But two important barriers lay close ahead. The first was the establishment of a common agricultural policy, and the second the move to closer political union once the treaty's provisions for majority voting in the Council of Ministers came into effect. The common agricultural policy presented practical difficulties, since it involved co-ordinating various national policies into a single European policy, rather than removing barriers altogether. Moreover, there were marked differences in efficiency in agriculture between the members of the Community—particularly between Germany and France; and farmers form a strong pressure group in all advanced Western countries. At the same time a common agricultural policy was linked to the question of closer political unity, since it would transfer one more function of government from national capitals to Brussels.

Such a development was fully in accordance with the aims and intentions of the Federalists, especially Jean Monnet and the Action Committee for United Europe. With the approach of majority voting in the Council of Ministers it looked as if the European institutions could be strengthened further and significant progress made towards political unity. The executives of the three communities—the High Authority of the Coal and Steel Community and the Commissions of Euratom and the Common Market—would be merged into a single European executive with a European budget. The merger of the three assemblies, which had already taken place, opened the way for a European Parliament in more than name—one directly elected by a European electorate.

The momentum of the Community and the ambitions of the Federalists provided a challenge for French policy. De Gaulle's own plans for closer union in Europe met with little success. His proposal for a confederation had not come into effect. Concrete proposals framed in 1961 (called the Fouchet Plan) for regular meetings of heads of state and ministers, backed up by commissions composed of national civil servants, had been shelved through lack of agreement amongst the other members of the Six. The Franco-German treaty, which formed part of the same concept, was in a troubled state. There was a direct conflict of interest between France and Germany, since de Gaulle wanted to sever ties with the United States, while Germany, so soon after the Berlin crisis, wanted to retain American support in Europe.

The failure of de Gaulle's own plans for a European confederal union—in which France would play a leading if not dominant part —was unlikely to induce him to accept political unity of the sort the Federalists wanted (with the possibility of France being outvoted in the Council of Ministers). At the same time he had no intention of breaking up the Common Market, from which France drew great benefit; and he was aware of the advantages which France would draw from an extension of its agricultural market—the more so since the efficiency of French agriculture had increased rapidly in the past decade.

The Commission had already grappled with the problem of

agriculture at the time of the negotiations with Britain. After the veto of January 1963 they had returned to the task and sought to show the continued vitality of the Community by resolving the difficulties which agriculture presented. The essence of their proposals lay in the establishment of a European fund which would be used as compensation for the losses any member would suffer as a result of a common agricultural policy. They also, following an established Community practice, agreed in principle that a single price should be fixed for certain agricultural products (of which wheat was the most important), and they agreed a date by which the actual price should be established. It was foreseen that price fixing would be harmful to farmers in the less efficient countries, particularly in Germany, since it would be lower than they had been accustomed to expect under a system of protection. It would have more general harmful effects in France where a higher price for wheat would have an inflationary impact on the economy as a whole. Both cases would justify compensation from the European fund which in turn would derive from a levy charged on agricultural imports from outside the Community. In this way those who bought from outside the Community at lower prices would contribute to the development o1 agricultural union within the Community.

In the best of circumstances a programme of this sort would have encountered difficulties. The Italians throughout 1964 imported an increased amount of food from outside the Community to meet the growing demand of a more prosperous industrial population. The German farmers reacted more sharply than their government had expected to the proposed fixing of prices for cereals. Their reaction was the more important since an election was due in the autumn of 1965 and the public opinion polls showed a sufficient number or "don't knows" to suggest that the Social Democrats might win fof the first time in the history of the Federal Republic.

Such difficulties were, however, of minor importance compared with the fact that the Commission hoped to use the advantages to France of an enlarged agricultural union as an inducement to persuade the French government to accept important moves towards political unity. Having surmounted one crisis over agriculture at the end of 1964 the Commission proposed in 1965 that the revenue coming into the agricultural fund, and from tariffs on other goods from outside the Community, should be at the disposal of the Community, which could then frame its own budget independent of national contributions. At the same time added powers would be given to the European Parliament by amendments to the Treaty of Rome.

If the Commission believed that such a proposal would be acceptable to de Gaulle they made a grave miscalculation. No advantage to France in the sale of cereals would be adequate to persuade him to accept political union of this sort. At the end of June 1965 France broke off negotiations, and withdrew its representatives from Brussels.

The whole momentum of the Community's development was thereby broken. It was impossible to imagine the Community without French participation—indeed the strength of de Gaulle's position lay in the fact that France was less dependent on the Common Market than the Common Market was on French participation. Germany was scarcely in a position to take over French leadership. It had done so to a limited extent after the first vote of January 1963 but its leadership was less acceptable to the smaller countries than was the French and unconvincing as long as the French were not there. Erhard, who had succeeded Adenauer as Chancellor, had his own reservations about the development towards political union. The country was preoccupied with the election, held in September 1965, which brought a substantial increase in the Social Democratic vote and, later, Social Democratic participation in the government. Germany thus lacked the dynamism and leadership to restore the Community's momentum: it was impossible for any of the smaller powers to do so.

Europe was thus in a state of suspense. The French withdrawal was only partial—the government did not revoke the Rome Treaty, nor did it go back on what had already been achieved in the setting up of the Common Market and the establishment of a common external tariff. Suspended animation of this kind could not last for very long. The long-term question of whether France and the Five should go their own separate ways, or whether some sort of compromise could be patched up would have to be faced. Meanwhile there were more immediate questions of a purely practical sort such as the Community's budget which had to be settled, and the Six had to decide what proposals they were prepared to make in the continuing negotiations for the "Kennedy round" of tariff reductions under GATT.

There were strong incentives towards agreement. The economic advantages already gained from the industrial Common Market were tangible and real. Equally important was the fact that, although it was the French who had deadlocked the Community's operations, de Gaulle and his government wanted a European policy—provided that it conformed to the General's view of the relations between states. Thus it was possible for the French government, like the other five, to press for a single Commission to replace the High Authority of the Coal and Steel Community and the Commissions of the Economic Community and Euratom. But while the European Federalists hoped in this way to move towards a supranational authority the French government wanted to weaken the High Authority of the Coal and Steel Community by absorbing it into the other two. As the Foreign Minister, Couve de Murville, said on 20 October 1965:

> the High Authority of the Coal and Steel Community . . . conceived in the romantic period, was an organization theoretically independent from the governments. Experience has shown the fallacy of such a system, and the wise men of the Common Market have been careful not to repeat the experiment. But this has not put an end to human temptation, as we have just seen.[1]

Thus, although the French government would rather go without the Community than accept supranationality, it supposed that a skilful combination of waiting for the right moment and then pressing its case with vigour would produce the kind of Community it wanted; and in this it was proved largely right.

[1] Speech before the National Assembly, Ambassade de France, *Bulletin Mensuel*, November 1965.

Representatives of the Six met together for the first time since the break of June 1965 in January 1966. They did not meet in Brussels—the home of the Community—since their intention was to decide whether the Community would resume its activities. Instead they met in Luxembourg, where the Coal and Steel Community has its headquarters. There a compromise was reached on the powers of the Community. The French pressed for a written agreement that majority voting would not be used in the Council of Ministers. The Five resisted such proposals, and above all were not prepared to modify the Treaty of Rome. But in the end they accepted a French statement to the effect that on matters concerning important interests of members of the Community discussion would continue until agreement was reached—and they incorporated this statement into their official record. On other points, too, compromise was reached. For example the French had wanted a written agreement that the Commission would not put up new proposals to the Council of Ministers without first having consulted governments. In the final agreement this proposal was watered down, and it was said that it was desirable that the Commission should "enter into contact" with the six governments.

Essentially the French had got their own way because the Five realized that unless they settled for a Community with more limited authority they might end up with no Community at all. The same was true with regard to the other topic which was discussed at Luxembourg—the timetable for the coming year. The French had always maintained that the breakdown of June 1965 had come because the others had not been prepared to agree on the establishment of the agricultural Common Market. They therefore argued that once agreement had been reached on the methods by which the Community worked and the powers of its component parts, the first problem for it to tackle must be that of agriculture. Only when this had been settled were they prepared to go on to consider the Community's policy towards the Kennedy round of tariff reductions.

In spite of the fact that the French stood to gain most in the immediate future from agreement on agriculture the Five accepted this timetable. As a result the Community was able to come to life again, and in February 1966 the first normal meeting since the break was held, and the Council of Ministers once more came together at Brussels. After the arduous discussions to which many of those concerned had now grown accustomed, two agreements of major importance were concluded on 11 May 1966 and 24 July 1966.

The agreements provided for the completion over the next few years of the Common Market in both agriculture and industry. The agreement on agriculture followed the lines already mapped out before June 1965. The Community took over responsibility for maintaining prices, for subsidizing farmers and growers, and for affecting major changes in the pattern of agricultural production to make it more efficient. Payment for the Community's activities was to come from the European Agricultural Guidance and Guarantee Fund, which in turn drew its money from member countries. Part of the payments into the Fund were made directly by governments out of their general budgets, and part from levies on imports from countries outside the Community. The payment out of the Fund going to each member country obviously depends on the level of agricultural production—the more that is produced the more is paid by the Fund to fill the gap between the artificially supported price and the world price at which exports can be sold. It was here that the advantage accruing to France is most obvious, particularly when compared with Germany. In 1967 France and Germany would each contribute just under one-third of the total for the Six in direct budgetary payments; but when the levies from imports were added to the budgetary contribution it was expected that Germany would pay 31 per cent and France only 24 per cent, and that Germany would receive only 18 per cent of the total out-payments from the Fund, compared with 45 per cent going to France.[1]

In order to compensate Germany for this advantage accruing to France it was agreed to speed up the movement towards a complete industrial Common Market. At first it looked as if this might be reached by the summer of 1967, but the French insisted that this would place too great a strain on their industries to meet foreign

[1] *Le Monde*, 12 May 1966.

competition. But minor concessions were made immediately to Germany, and in addition it was agreed that the entire customs union should be complete by 1 July 1968—a year and a half earlier than the Treaty of Rome had provided. By that time, if no interruption occurred, the six members of the Community would enjoy free trade between themselves, and have the same tariff to the outside world.

What, then, was the balance of forces established after this new compromise between the demands of French nationalism and the force of European union? On the one hand it appeared that de Gaulle had succeeded in giving a new shape to the European institutions, closely corresponding to his own political outlook; on the other hand the striking fact emerged that the European Economic Community had emerged from the crisis—and indeed had made progress—in spite of the concessions made to France. The original *élan* of public feeling about Europe had weakened since the great days of the European movement and nationalism had reasserted itself under the leadership of France and de Gaulle. On the other hand the institutions of Europe existed, and had developed a degree of integration which many would regard as more likely to endure than passing enthusiasm.

For no country was the question of the future more important than for Britain. In October 1964 a Labour government was once again returned to power in Britain, and in March 1966 it fought a further election which brought it a substantial majority. The coolness which the Labour party had traditionally shown towards Europe persisted in some sections of the party; but the government was increasingly aware of the same sort of considerations which had led its Conservative predecessor to seek admission to Europe. Economic conditions in Britain continued to be a major preoccupation. Economic growth was slow, prices rose more than wages, and there was a continuing crisis over the balance of payments. Up to a point these problems had to be solved within a national framework. It was a question of increasing productivity and holding wages and prices down so that Britain maintained its competitive position abroad, and it was a question of doing away with restrictive practices, making greater use of technological resources, and improving marketing in order to compete successfully in the export market.

But in addition the British government was aware of the large market across the Channel. Proposals for a Channel tunnel were now being given serious consideration—but it was no good making an easy way under the Channel if the barrier of customs duties still remained. This was a long-term argument. Economic analysis showed that entry to the Common Market would increase Britain's difficulties initially by adding to the problem of the balance of payments and by bringing an increase in the price of foodstuffs. Calculation of economic advantage therefore depended on forecasts of factors difficult to measure, such as the opportunities offered by a larger market and the impact of competition. Moreover, economic considerations were subordinate to political. The Prime Minister and some of his colleagues saw the danger of Britain being excluded from so large a political unit as the Common Market. The danger was great enough with the limited degree of co-operation possible under French dominance. It would increase if there were greater political unity—or if French dominance were succeeded by German.

For Britain, Europe was still a reflex from the Commonwealth. As the colonies had been given their independence the Commonwealth had become increasingly an ideal for the Labour party, because it represented a unique form of co-operation between developed and developing countries, between the black races and the white. But the African members of the Commonwealth were going through a period which caused disillusion to some, and positive embarrassment to the Labour government. The two west African countries on which high hopes had been placed—Ghana and Nigeria—underwent violent political disorder. Nigeria was one of the African countries on which most hope had been placed at the time of its independence, and until 1966 it had appeared to live up to these hopes in terms of its democratic government and internal stability. Its near neighbour, Ghana, in contrast, had for some years given the appearance of corrupt and authoritarian government until, in February 1966, some of its army officers followed the Nigerian example and overthrew the government of Kwame Nkrumah—after which the Ghanaians themselves revealed the full extent of the decay which had fastened itself on their country.

Political upheaval in west Africa weakened Commonwealth ties. So did the British government's experience with the problems of Rhodesia. As Southern Rhodesia this country had enjoyed almost complete independence from Britain since 1923, but its own government had remained in the hands of the small European minority of the population. Before taking the final steps towards complete independence the British government wanted to persuade the Rhodesians to accept a new constitution which would ensure that the black Africans would have a majority in the government. But the Rhodesians would not be persuaded, and in November 1965 declared their independence—a "unilateral declaration of independence"—without any further constitutional change which would threaten their position.

The British government was not prepared to give in to the Rhodesians, led by Ian Smith; on the other hand there were no very effective measures which it could bring against them. It would have been extremely difficult to use force, and there did not appear to be an alternative Rhodesian government to put in power even if force was successfully used; it could only apply sanctions, but it was sceptical about the results of sanctions—especially since they might cause complications with Rhodesia's neighbour, South Africa, which was one of Britain's most important trading partners. The African states were in no position to help Britain and Rhodesia's northern neighbour, Zambia, later suffered from a policy of sanctions more than did Rhodesia itself; yet they pressed Britain to take action of some sort, and not to allow a new state based on the supremacy of its white minority to come into existence.

It was in these circumstances that the Labour government, like its Conservative predecessor, came to the conclusion that it must explore the possibilities of entry into Europe. The Commonwealth was a bed of thorns, and certainly lacked any strength or cohesion as a political force compared with the Common Market across the

Channel. Not only that but the government saw—as Churchill had seen twenty years earlier—that only in some sort of combination could Europe hope to compete with the United States in technological development. And although the British continued to express unequivocally its support for and association with the United States —an unpopular position with some members of the Labour party because of the Vietnam War—it must also have had in mind the possibility of American politics moving in such a way that Britain would want greater political pull in its relations with the United States.

Harold Wilson announced to the House of Commons on 10 November 1966 that the government had decided to make a new "high-level approach" to see whether conditions existed for fruitful negotiations on British membership of the European Economic Community.

As Britain set about its second attempt to join western Europe the atmosphere in Europe as a whole had completely changed, even from what it had been a few years previously. The Economic Community had survived the onslaught of de Gaulle's nationalism, even though its movement towards greater supranationalism had been stopped. NATO had changed in a more fundamental way. De Gaulle insisted that France remain a member of the North Atlantic alliance—signed in 1949 for a period of twenty years—and would look for a renewal of the Treaty in 1969. But at the same time he described the system of integration of commands and armies, which for the other members were an essential part of the whole structure of the alliance, as "subordination". This subordination, he said in a press conference in September 1965, must come to an end by 1969 at the latest. The following March he went further in saying that France must regain complete sovereignty over its territory— "which", he said, "at present is impaired by the permanent presence of allied military elements or by the habitual use being made of her air-space".[1] As a result the other members of the alliance had no choice but to remove, expensive as it was to do so, the headquarters from France to Belgium, and to accept the fact that France

[1] Message to President Lyndon Johnson, 7 March 1966; Ambassade de France, *Bulletin Mensuel*, April 1966.

would no longer take part in combined NATO forces—although the French government expressed its willingness to discuss the combination of its forces with NATO forces in the event of war.

The French attitude to NATO followed from de Gaulle's beliefs about national sovereignty and about the importance of nuclear weapons in modern strategy. He therefore believed that it would be folly to entrust either a supranational organization of the sort intended for the Economic Community, or an alliance structure like NATO with any decision of any importance to the nation. Decisions which affected national interests, far more national survival, could only be taken by national governments.

First and foremost, therefore, national governments, and they alone, must be responsible for defence. This had always been true, and had been more so with the development of nuclear weapons and missiles. De Gaulle did not believe that there was any immediate prospect of war in Europe. But if some improbable development were to bring an outbreak of war, then nuclear weapons would very quickly be brought into play. A situation could then exist when the United States would avoid an attack on itself provided that it did not defend Europe. In such a situation the obligations which the United States had assumed under the North Atlantic Treaty would not be strong enough to persuade an American President to launch nuclear weapons from the United States on the Soviet Union, thus invoking self-destruction. For this reason even more than before France must be responsible for its own defence, including the maintenance of its own nuclear deterrent—not as strong as that of the Soviet Union, but sufficiently strong to be a credible deterrent.

The French view was diametrically opposed to that of its allies in most respects. Even they had found no means to give control over nuclear weapons to anything other than national governments. But in all other matters of defence—including the deployment of nuclear weapons, short of their actually being used—they believed that nations had been weak in the past precisely because they had retained their complete independence, and had not been ready to combine to ward off an attack. They were well aware of the shortcomings of military campaigns in previous wars when men fighting the same battle were under separate national commanders with different national equipment and different communications systems. They saw that in both the world wars of the twentieth century a single supreme command had had to be established, and they maintained that this should be done in advance of any possible war—together with all the accompaniment of common weapons, communications, equipment of all sorts. It was this which they called "integration", while de Gaulle called it "subordination".

At the same time their estimate of the chances of war in Europe was the same as de Gaulle's. They did not think it a likely eventuality, and they thought that if war did start it would quickly become a nuclear war. No government now imagined—in the mid-1960's— that the Soviet Union was going to launch an all-out attack in western Europe. Nor did they think that there was any danger of a limited attack in the centre of Europe of the sort people had once discussed—say a lightning thrust to capture Hamburg. Least of all did they think that a war would begin through some kind of accident, such as Soviet troops getting lost across the zonal border in Germany. It was always possible for Soviet policy to change, and for Russia to take up a threatening attitude or to plan some attack in Europe; but they were confident that such a change would be preceded by plentiful indications in changed Soviet policies for them to be able to prepare against it.

In this way NATO had changed quite independently of the withdrawal of France from its organization. The North Atlantic Treaty had been signed in the heat of crisis, at the time of the Czech *coup* and the Berlin blockade, and it had been armed and equipped under the impact of the Korean War. The new Czech crisis of 1968 was interpreted differently from that of twenty years earlier. Brutal as Soviet action was, it was not thought to be the prelude to advance into western Europe. While the Russian occupation of Czecho-slovakia thus reaffirmed the necessity of NATO as a defensive organization, it was not thought of as countering an immediate threat to the security of western Europe.

# CHAPTER 8

# The New Europe?

FROM the other side of what used to be thought of as the Iron Curtain, Communist governments saw the economic challenge of the Common Market and EFTA. When Khrushchev had spoken of the disappearance of the inevitability of war between the Socialist and the Imperialist worlds he had also talked of "competitive co-existence"—confident that Socialist planning would overtake capitalism. The next year the EEC Treaty was signed, and just as the conclusion of the WEU agreement was matched by the signing of the Warsaw Treaty, so a major attempt was made to strengthen Comecon—a process started in 1956 and interrupted by the events of the autumn.

There were major differences between the problems confronting the eastern European states and those of their western counterparts. The extent of organized co-operation and integration was not automatically defined. It could be argued that all Communist states should be included—Cuba, North Vietnam, China, North Korea, Outer Mongolia, as well as Russia and the eastern European countries, and the attempt was made to bring these states in. It failed as far as China was concerned for political reasons; it was only of marginal importance for the others for practical reasons. Cuba had an interest in standardization of sizes and patterns in the Communist bloc, but much less in co-ordinated investment since it was geographically so remote.

The practical tasks of co-operation were very different from those between the modern Capitalist societies of the West. The industrial sector of the Common Market rested on private industry, with a small public component in the nationalized industries (which, nonetheless, ran commercially). Although this predominantly private enterprise was governed by regulations and orders, and although its activities were affected by government economic and social policies it remained essentially a free-enterprise arrangement, and the first task of the EEC had been to remove barriers. On the Communist side, in contrast, the whole of the industrial economy of importance to integration was nationalized, and investment and output were determined by governmental decision rather than by the price mechanism. The establishment of an integrated economy was bound to be a more complicated task. It consisted of establishing joint international or intergovernmental machinery to plan production in several independent countries, rather than the removal of barriers. Moreover the development of Comecon for this purpose was taking place at exactly the time when the Soviet Union and other Communist countries were giving greater initiative to factory managers and placing more reliance on the price mechanism. The pull between these two forces, the one towards centralized planning and the other towards decentralized decision-making was bound to cause tension.

A further practical difficulty arose from the disproportion in the eastern European states created by the participation of the Soviet Union—in contrast to the comparative detachment of the United States. In the years of the Marshall Plan the United States had been closely involved in western European planning and had provided the resources for it. Thereafter it had withdrawn from economic co-operation—except for OECD, which was not confined to Europe. Private investment flowed into western Europe, the United States worked for the reduction of tariffs in GATT, and in a number of ways it remained close to western Europe. But EEC and EFTA developed independently.

The geographical contiguity of the Soviet Union to eastern Europe made a parallel detachment of Russia from eastern Europe impracticable—nor would the Soviet leaders be likely to favour the growth of a Comecon, with the cohesion of EEC, outside their control. There was a minor theme to the dominance of Russia. By world standards all of the countries of eastern Europe are at a roughly equal level of development; but within their own context there are marked differences between the degree of industrial development in Poland (including the whole of Silesia) and Rumania.

However, these difficulties were unimportant compared with the great political storms which swept across the Communist world at the very time when it seemed most desirable to develop economic co-operation. The centre of the storm was the Sino-Soviet dispute, which rose to a crescendo at the end of the fifties and only quietened —without in any way being resolved—as a result of an even more searing dispute within China itself. The issues of the dispute were not themselves of direct consequence to the countries of eastern Europe. China's aspirations to nuclear power, its wish to be recognized as the pre-eminent power in Asia, did not affect their immediate future. The economic development of China was remote from their own problems. But the Soviet Union looked to the other Communist parties of the world for support against China, and this support they could give or withhold. Albania gave strong support to the Chinese position and espoused its cause. Rumania flirted with the Chinese to strengthen its position in relation to the Soviet Union. But throughout the vital years in the strengthening of Comecon the Sino-Soviet dispute wasted and dissipated energy.

In spite of these difficulties the achievements of the new co-operation were considerable. There was a great increase in trade within Comecon—more than doubling between 1955 and 1962.[1] The Communist countries enjoyed an advantage over the Capitalists in that there were no "trade secrets"—technological expertise was readily available to other Socialist enterprises, and Comecon offices facilitated the exchange of technical data and information about new processes. Some progress was made towards the specialization of member countries in particular products. Moreover, when a general agreement covering the whole of Comecon could not be reached, negotiations nonetheless often contributed to a growing network of bilateral agreements.

[1] See KASER, *Comecon*, p. 123.

In one respect eastern Europe might seem to be like the west: the integration of Comecon was accompanied by the growth of vigorous nationalism in one country, Rumania. There had been no upheaval in Rumania in 1956 similar to that which shook Poland and Hungary, and the government kept close control of its people. At the same time it came to assert more and more strongly its sovereignty and independence, and to resist any proposals which would limit them. By 1964 the Rumanians took the position that they would leave Comecon if it pursued any supranational objectives, stating that "transmitting such levers to the competence of superstate or extra-state bodies would turn sovereignty into a notion without content."[1] Even more striking was the fact that in the same year, at the United Nations Conference on Trade and Development, the Rumanian delegate made a parallel with the prewar years, thus appealing to a national tradition anterior to Rumania's present-day communism. He said:

> The Rumanian People's Republic consistently strives for the promotion of normal economic relations among all the states of the world, irrespective of their social system, based on strict observance of national sovereignty, economic independence, equality in rights and non-interference in domestic affairs. I should like to recall that at a European economic conference held thirty years ago, the Rumanian representative expressed his hope that the day would come when an international conference would discuss the various aspects of world economy.[2]

In this way Rumania clearly situated itself as an independent state, pursuing its own economic interests within a world framework, rather than one member of a Communist group. In doing so it was to some extent following a Yugoslav lead. Yugoslavia had never come back into the Communist fold after the break, for the reconciliation of 1956 was only partial. It participated in Comecon activities, but at the same time was an observer member of OECD, and also applied for an association with the Common Market. It participated in the Communist and non-Communist world in accordance with its own national interests.

[1] *Ibid.*, p. 94.
[2] *Ibid.*, p. 103.

A decisive change had thus come about in the Communist world. The founder of communism, Karl Marx, had abandoned his Prussian nationality in his youth and remained "stateless" until his death. He saw nationalism and the nation state as a thing of the past. He believed that the bonds binding men together were those of class rather than the nation, and he saw the development of communism as the creation of a world community. As he wrote in the *Communist Manifesto*:

> In the place of the old wants, satisfied by the production of the country, we find new wants, requiring for their satisfaction the products of distant lands and climes. In place of the old local and national self-exclusion and self-sufficiency, we have intercourse in every direction, universal inter-dependence of nations. And as in material, so also in intellectual production. The intellectual creations of individual nations become common property. National one-sidedness and narrow-mindedness become more impossible, and from the numerous national and local literatures there arises a world literature.

The establishment of a Communist society would take this development further towards the elimination of national divisions.

Stalin, dominating the Communist world for thirty years, created a system which made it impossible for national aspirations to show themselves—but not in the way Marx had expected. Stalin was not an internationalist but a Russian nationalist. The unity which he imposed on the Communist world was one where the learning of Russian was compulsory in the countries of eastern Europe and where the architectural style of government buildings in a southern capital like Bucharest was that of similar buildings in Moscow.

By successive stages the Stalinist system had been dismantled—by Krushchev's attack on Stalin, the dissolution of the Cominform, the intrusion of the Sino-Soviet dispute into the relations between the Communist parties of Europe. The Communist states now had control over their own governments and could shape their own domestic policies and, to a certain extent, their foreign policies. (In March 1968 the Syrian Communist party leader vigorously attacked the Rumanians for their attitude to the Middle East War of the preceding summer at a meeting of Communist parties in Budapest

—and the Rumanians walked out of the conference when they failed to receive adequate apologies.)

Nationalism and the organization of the nation state had thus reasserted their importance, and there was no obvious way in which the close cohesion of earlier days could be reimposed. The Comintern and the Cominform were both discredited. The methods of terror which Stalin had employed were removed from the Soviet system—even though the police retained arbitrary powers and intellectual freedom was suppressed. The ideological unity of the Communist world was a thing of the past. Ever since 1948 the Yugoslavs had insisted on their own road to socialism, and twenty years later it was accepted that no one Communist party or state had any right to dictate ideological tenets to the others. The success of the Communist system in Russia was no longer unique now that there was a multiplicity of Communist states, each of them having a Nationalist pride in its own achievement. Periodic meetings of Communist parties designed to affirm and elaborate a certain degree of unity inevitably suffered from dissension and disagreement amongst representatives, and the question of China was a constantly disturbing element.

The changed relationship between the states of the Communist world was accompanied by the development of their contacts with the West. The Soviet Union led the way in this process. Its position in international politics brought it into close contact with the West, however tense its relationships might be. The United States was its chief rival—but it was also the one other power of comparable size with which it had to establish an understanding and a *modus vivendi*. In order not to fall behind in technological development it sought to strengthen and extend contacts which would improve its expertise and resources. In this way it could hope to eliminate the unevenness of its development—having primacy in some area of space research while remaining lamentably behind in others.

The smaller countries of eastern Europe were ready in varying degrees to follow suit. Many of them, Poland and Rumania in particular, had historic ties with western Europe, especially with France. Moreover there were practical incentives for the eastern

European states to pursue outside interests. By selling outside Comecon they could acquire foreign exchange, and this was useful in any form of trade. A favourable balance of hard currencies from outside the Soviet bloc gave flexibility to a country's economy which was harder to achieve through the bureaucratic exchange agreements of Comecon. Thus, while the increase in trade within Comecon was impressive, there were examples of east–west trade which were far more so. The trade of France and Rumania was only just over a million pounds when it was resumed in 1954; by 1963 it was nearly twenty million—Rumania's chief export to France being refined petroleum products.

The countries of western Europe were eager to seek new markets in the east, both in the smaller countries and in the Soviet Union itself. In many areas of mass production the Soviet Union could still draw with advantage on Western technology. They therefore signed an agreement with Fiat to establish a motor-car factory in Russia, and agreements with Britain for the establishment of synthetic fibre plants. In other fields exchange of technical knowledge was instituted—in agricultural co-operation, and, in 1967, with Britain in aircraft construction. Meanwhile the volume of east–west trade increased. The United States government attached sufficient importance to this development to want to participate in it, but encountered the obstacle of congressional opposition to trade with Communist countries. Even so it took the important step of raising its legations to the status of embassies.

France took the lead in constructing a closer relationship with the countries of eastern Europe. It was an integral part of de Gaulle's policy to do so. He had deliberately separated France from the alliance with America—although still adhering to the Atlantic treaty—and was fiercely critical of American policy, especially in Vietnam. He believed that in so far as Europe should be united at all, it should be "from the Atlantic to the Urals"—a concept vague at the edges, but clearly transcending the barriers created by Communist ideology. The Rumanian appeal to traditions of the 1930's readily struck an echoing chord in France, since French policy was historically based on a relationship with eastern Europe.

From 1964 onwards a series of visits were exchanged between France on the one hand and the Soviet Union, Bulgaria, Rumania, and Yugoslavia on the other. The exchanges, which extended to the other countries of the Communist bloc even when there were no ministerial visits, were of economic and political importance. They resulted in trade agreements and political discussion, sometimes the raising of the status of the diplomatic mission from legation to embassy. They culminated in the most moving of them all—the visit of de Gaulle to Poland in September 1967. It was forty years since he had gone there as a young captain after the First World War. It was twenty years since western Europe had rushed to unite, its Catholic élite amongst others taking the lead in defence against communism; now de Gaulle celebrated his reunion with Poland by taking Mass in Warsaw cathedral—and the photograph of the ceremony was circulated by the Polish press agency in Poland.

De Gaulle's Polish visit did little to improve French relations with Germany. De Gaulle stated clearly that Polish frontiers must remain unchanged—and thereby include territory which some Germans thought of as the "lost provinces", and which the German Federal government did not want to concede in advance of negotiations in which it might hope to gain something in return. But the development in German policy was as significant as that of France. The German Federal Republic had always refused to establish diplomatic relations with any Communist country—except the Soviet Union. This policy had come to be known as the Hallstein Doctrine, and it followed from the statement the German government made in 1955 that it would regard recognition of the government of the Democratic Republic as an "unfriendly act", and would not therefore recognize any government that established relations with East Germany. Ten years later the price of this policy was that the Germans saw the French establishing themselves in powerful positions, trading and diplomatic, in an area close to Germany and one of traditional importance to them. At the beginning of 1967 the Hallstein Doctrine was abandoned, and diplomatic relations established with Rumania. With other eastern European countries trade agreements had already been signed.

By the middle of the 1960's some of the old patterns of Europe had thus re-emerged. The personality of such states as Rumania, Hungary and Poland was clearly visible, and they had re-established historic ties with the West. Paradoxically it looked as if the reappearance of nationalism might give a new meaning to the unity of Europe.

But it is important not to exaggerate the scale of these developments. The trade of western European countries, and even more of the United States, with the East was still a very small proportion of their total trade. Politically the problem of Germany remained.

Communist rule in eastern Europe had become less tyrannical than in the early days and the harsh dividing-line between east and west had become very much easier to cross. But the apparatus of Communist rule, the single-party state and the police system, the suppression of intellectual and political freedom, had not disappeared. The Iron Curtain had become very much easier for westerners to penetrate to visit the east of Europe—with strict limitations once they entered the Soviet Union—but travel in the reverse direction was only marginally easier for the ordinary citizens of Communist countries. Meanwhile the dividing-line was straddled by the political problems of a severed Germany.

The narrow limits within which Communist states were circumscribed were made startlingly evident in the experience of Czechoslovakia in 1968. In the spring of that year the Communist party of Czechoslovakia initiated an unprecedented programme of liberalization; in the summer it was brutally ended when Soviet troops occupied the country in a full-scale invasion such as had not occurred since the liberation of the territory from the German armies.

Economic reform had begun in Czechoslovakia in the preceding year; it was brought into effect after considerable enquiry and discussion of the reasons for poor agricultural output and shortcomings in industrial exports, leading to severe shortage of foreign exchange. The changes introduced in January 1967 reduced the role of the State in detailed planning and gave greater scope to the managers of individual enterprises, whose performance would be judged by their ability to sell their products at a profit.

Whatever effect liberalization of this sort might have on the economy of the country, it was unlikely to assuage the demands which were being made for political change.Writers and intellectuals demanded greater freedom and the removal of restrictions on the press (which had actually been increased when the economic reforms were introduced); at the same time, there was a struggle within the leadership of the Communist party for the removal of Antonin Novotny, who had been First Secretary since 1953 and President of the Republic since 1957. The sense of upheaval in the country was increased by a student demonstration in Prague at the end of October, followed by strong criticisms of police brutality voiced by the staff of the University.

These events came to a head in January 1968 when Novotny was removed from the secretaryship of the party and Alexander Dubcek was appointed in his place. But this change was only the beginning of more far-reaching and fundamental developments. A few months later Novotny—who was now accused of favouritism in the army—was ousted from the Presidency and replaced by General Svoboda. Significantly Svoboda's election was by secret ballot. Restrictions on the press and on the import of foreign newspapers were abolished. Ministers and officials associated with the old policy resigned or were removed from office. A formal apology to the students of Prague University for the behaviour of the police was broadcast. The Prime Minister resigned and was replaced by Oldrich Cernik.

The new leadership proceeded to announce sweeping plans for the establishment of what it called "socialist democracy". The government explicitly rejected any form of "non-socialist" democracy, but discussed the role of the Communist party in terms which no Communists had used before. In its "Action Programme" of April 1968 the Communist party said:

> The leading role of the party was too often understood in the past as a monopolistic concentration of power in the hands of the party organs. . . . This weakened the initiative and responsibilities of the State and of economic and social institutions, damaged the authority of the party, and made it impossible for the party to fulfil its basic tasks. The party must fight . . . for the voluntary support of a majority within the framework of the democratic rules of a socialist State. . . .[1]

[1] *Keesing's Contempory Archives* (1968), p. 22713

Political freedoms were immediately introduced. The changed political atmosphere was demonstrated when the Communist newspaper *Rude Pravo* conducted a questionnaire amongst its readers about the position of the ruling Communist party in the context of democracy.

The new freedoms were accompanied by enquiry into the events of the past, shrouded in silence until now. The enquiry extended to the death, immediately after the *coup d'état* of February 1948, of Jan Masaryk—attributed at the time to suicide, but always with the suspicion of murder. The trials of the 1950's were also called into account. As these enquiries proceeded, no fewer than four high-ranking officials committed suicide.

The extent and nature of these changes were unprecedented in any Communist country. They were carried out by the leadership of the party itself, and although they were made in the context of student demands and general intellectual unrest it could not be said that they were in response to popular revolt. They were warmly received by the people of Czechoslovakia, who welcomed the strong current of freedom of a sort they had not known for twenty years.

To the same degree they aroused feelings of hope—and foreboding —outside Czechoslovakia. For reformers in the other countries of the Soviet bloc—some of them powerful within their own governments—new possibilities of liberalization seemed to be opening up, while in western Europe Gaullist policy appeared vindicated. But in eastern Europe the Czech liberalization aroused fears as well as hopes, for in countries like Poland and Hungary it was difficult to see where such liberalization would end once it was allowed to start.

Even more was this the case in the Soviet Union itself. Over a period of fifty years the Communist leadership of that country had established a system of government whose central object was to keep power in its own hands. Moreover, Russian Communist government, with all the apparatus of a modern totalitarian state, was the successor to an absolute monarchy more resistant to reform than any other in Europe. The ideas of the Czech reformers were a direct threat and challenge to such a government.

It is not surprising, therefore, that there were constant meetings between the Russian and Czech leaders, as well as meetings amongst the leaders of the other eastern European states—meetings, however, to which the Rumanians were not invited. By the early part of the summer it appeared that the Soviet Union was conducting a war of nerves against the Czechs to oblige them to withdraw from the movement of liberalization. The Czechs expressed their determination to remain within the socialist camp and gave their assurances to their eastern allies—without making any practical concessions. The Russians were in a position to strangle the economy of the country; more alarming, Russian troops took part in Warsaw Pact manoeuvres in Czechoslovakia, and lingered there after the manoeuvres were over.

When they at last withdrew it seemed that the Czechs might succeed in carrying a long stage further the process of national independence linked with liberalization which had made its start in the other satellite countries. Then, on the night of 20 August 1968 the Soviet Union launched a full-scale invasion of Czechoslovakia with its own troops and those of Poland, East Germany, and Hungary. The occupation was a large-scale military enterprise, in which some half-million troops were involved.

Czech armed forces made no attempt to resist the invasion, but the occupying forces were everywhere met by the hostility of the people, who sometimes did all they could to impede the progress of the armies, and suffered casualties as a result. The radio and television services were also effective centres of opposition. As the invasion took place clandestine stations sprang into existence in numerous parts of the country, and when occupation was complete the satire of the Czech television was kept up to form a rearguard action against the Russians.

The occupation put an end to and indeed reversed the process of liberalization in Czechoslovakia, but it could not restore the Communist world to its old Stalinist pattern. As long as Dubcek and Cernik stayed in power (although at the time of writing it was impossible to foresee how long this would be) they formed a Czechoslovak government enjoying the support of the people against the Russians. They were not, as the Stalinist rulers had been, the creatures of the Russians, but neither were they free agents. They were left no choice but to reappoint conservatives who had been dismissed and to re-establish censorship. The Soviet troops remained in the country. But the Czechs clung to the control of the government of their country in spite of occupation and although subject to constant Russian pressure.

Nor did the occupation of Czechoslovakia restore the unity of the Communist world. Rumania was strongly opposed to Russian action, although forced to adopt a cautious position in view of its own vulnerability to similar invasion. In the west, European Communist parties were thrown off balance by the news of Russian action; although still linked to Moscow, they had been improving their domestic position by behaving as ordinary democratic parties —the French Communist party had made a working alliance with the socialist and other left-wing parties. Instead of tamely following a party line laid down in Moscow, as they would have done twenty years earlier, these parties now condemned Russian action in Czechoslovakia.

In the face of such criticism the Soviet government offered a systematic justification for its actions. At a meeting of the Polish Communist party in November 1968 Brezhnev (the First Secretary of the Russian Communist party) said that the invasion of Czechoslovakia was "an extraordinary step, dictated by necessity" and generalized from the events of the summer by saying:

> when internal and external forces that are hostile to socialism try to turn the development of some socialist country towards the restoration of a capitalist regime, when socialism in that country and the socialist community as a whole are threatened, it becomes not only a problem of the country concerned, but a common problem and concern of all socialist countries.

The implications of such a doctrine for a country like Rumania were obvious enough, while in Yugoslavia Tito's government expressed renewed alarm about the possibility of Soviet intervention there. But at the same time the fact that such a declaration had to be made at all showed how the hold of the Soviet Union on eastern

Europe had changed—such justification would not have been thought necessary in Stalin's day.

The occupation slowed down and hindered the development of contacts between East and West. De Gaulle was vigorous in his condemnation of Russian action. But it did not bring any major intensification of the cold war. The Soviet Ambassador called on the American Secretary of State on the day of the invasion to explain his country's action, and the American reaction made it clear that it recognized tacitly a division of Europe into spheres of influence. The United States government did not intend that the new coup in Czechoslovakia should impede the movement towards relaxation of tension between the two super powers, and it sought to press ahead with the ratification of a treaty for the non-proliferation of nuclear weapons—and keep the channels to Moscow open on the question of Vietnam.

By the end of 1968, therefore, Europe appeared to be stationary. In western Europe the movement towards unity was "in the doldrums"; between East and West the growing contacts and restoration of historic ties was cut back by Soviet action in Czechoslovakia. But the experience of the decades since the war left no reason to suppose that this period of rest would last very long before the forces of unity and nationalism reasserted themselves to disturb this unstable equilibrium.

# Selective Reading List

ARON, R. and LERNER, D., *France defeats EDC*, London, Thames & Hudson, 1957.

BEAUFFRE, A., *Deterrence and Strategy*, London, Faber & Faber, 1965.

BELOFF, M., *Europe and the Europeans*, London, Chatto & Windus, 1957.

BELOFF, M., *The United States and the Unity of Europe*, London, Faber & Faber, 1963.

BELOFF, N., *The General says No*, Harmondsworth, Penguin Books, 1963.

BRZEZINSKI, Z., *The Soviet Bloc: Unity and Conflict*, New York, Praeger, 1960.

CALLEO, D., *Europe's Future*, London, Hodder & Stoughton, 1967.

CAMPS, M., *Britain and the European Community*, London, OUP, 1964.

CAMPS, M., *European Unification in the 1960s*, London, OUP, 1967.

CHATHAM HOUSE and PEP, European Series, London, 1967– . 1, *Concentration of Competition*. 2, *Europe and the Developing World*. 3, *Agriculture, the Cost of Joining the Common Market*. 4, *The Sterling Problem and the Six*. 5, *Planning in the EEC*. 6, *Taxes in the EEC and Britain*. 7, *Towards a European Civil Service*. 8, *The Institutions of the European Community*.

CLAY, L. DU B., *Decision in Germany*, London, Heinemann, 1950.

DJILAS, M., *Conversations with Stalin*, London, Rupert Hart Davis, 1962.

ECONOMIST INTELLIGENCE UNIT, *The Commonwealth and Europe*, London, *The Economist*, 1960.

FREYMOND, J., *The Saar Conflict, 1945–55*, London, Stevens, 1960.

FREYMOND, J., *Western Europe since the War*, London, Pall Mall, 1964.

GAULLE, C. DE, *War Memoirs*. 1, *The Call to Honour*. 2, *Unity*. 3, *Salvation*. London, Weidenfeld & Nicolson, 1959–60.

GAULLE, C. DE, *Major Addresses*, London, French Embassy, 1964.

GROSSER, A., *The Federal Republic of Germany*, London, Pall Mall, 1964.

HAAS, E. B., *The Uniting of Europe*, London, Stevens, 1958.

HALLSTEIN, W., *United Europe*, Cambridge, Mass., Harvard UP, 1962.

HAYES, C. J. H., *The Historical Evolution of Modern Nationalism*, New York, 1931.

HUDSON, G., *The Hard and Bitter Peace*, London, Pall Mall, 1966.

KASER, M., *Comecon*, 2nd ed., OUP, London, 1967.

KENNAN, G., *American Diplomacy, 1900–1950*, Chicago UP, 1951.

KENNAN, G., *Memoirs*, London, 1968.

KISSINGER, H., *Troubled Partnership*, New York, McGraw-Hill, 1965.

KITZINGER, U., *The Challenge of the Common Market*, Oxford, Blackwell, 1962.

KNAPP, W., *A History of War and Peace, 1939–65*, London, OUP, 1967.

KOHN, H., *Nationalism: its History and Meaning*, Princeton UP, 1965.

LAQUEUR, W. and LABEDZ, L. (Eds.), *Polycentrism*, London, Pall Mall, 1962.

LINDBERG, L. N., *The Political Dynamics of European Economic Integration.*

LIPPMANN, W., *The Cold War*, New York, Harper, 1947.

MACKINTOSH, J. M., *The Strategy and Tactics of World Communism*, London, OUP, 1962.

MOORE, B., *NATO and the Future of Europe*, New York, Harper, 1958.

NAMIER, L., *Nationality and Liberty in Avenues of History*, London, Hamish Hamilton, 1952.

OSGOOD, R., *NATO the Entangling Alliance*, Chicago UP, 1962.

PICKLES, W., *Not with Europe; The Political Case for Staying Out*, London, Fabian Society, 1962.

PICKLES, W., *How Much has Changed?*, Oxford, Blackwell, 1967.

PRICE, H. B., *The Marshall Plan and its Meaning*, New York, Cornell UP, 1955.

ROBERTSON, A. H., *European Institutions*, 2nd edn., New York, Praeger, 1966.

ROYAL INSTITUTE OF INTERNATIONAL AFFAIRS, *Soviet Yugoslav Dispute*, London, OUP, 1948.

SETON-WATSON, H., *The East European Revolution*, London, Methuen, 1956.

SETON-WATSON, H., *Neither War nor Peace*, London, Methuen, 1960.

ULAM, A. B., *Titoism and the Cominform*, Cambridge, Mass., Harvard UP, 1952.

WALTER, I., *The European Common Market*, New York, Praeger, 1967.

# *Index*